Bragging About GOD Again:

Holy Spirit Encounters

JONI JONES

XULON ELITE

Xulon Press Elite
2301 Lucien Way #415
Maitland, FL 32751
407.339.4217
www.xulonpress.com

Scripture quotations taken from the New King James Version (NKJV). Copyright © 1979, 1980, 1982 by Thomas Nelson, Inc. Used by permission. All rights reserved.

Scripture quotations taken from the English Standard Version (ESV). Copyright © 2001 by Crossway, a publishing ministry of Good News Publishers. Used by permission. All rights reserved.

Scripture quotations taken from the Holy Bible, New Living Translation (NLT). Copyright ©1996, 2004, 2007 by Tyndale House Foundation. Used by permission of Tyndale House Publishers, Inc.

Printed in the United States of America.

ISBN-13: 9781498480185

Preface

A Love Story

While praying early in the morning, I was thanking God, "Thank You, Lord, for my God stories and…"

Before I finished my sentence the Holy Spirit, (the Spirit), spoke over me, "They are not YOUR God stories, they are OUR MEMORIES!"

God's comment took my breath away. My eyes welled with tears at this intimate revelation that He and I have partnered together working side-by-side since before my fifth birthday. We worked together to accomplish His plans with extraordinary results.

Simply put, I am prophetic and a seer. God gives me dreams, visions, speaks to me, gives me strong feelings deep inside and many times I just know things. Upon occasion, I have seen into the spiritual realm and have interacted with angels and I have seen and dealt with demons.

Trying to understand who I am because of these gifts has been a life-long process and very confusing for me as well as others around me. When walking under the direction of the Spirit, I am given instructions on what to do, where to go and what to say.

For we know in part and we prophecy in part. (1 Corinthians 13:9)

The one question that runs through the minds of prophetic people and people who don't realize that God speaks to them is, *Did I just make this up?* Trust me, we've all had those thoughts. Those who know exactly what I mean and those who want to understand the spiritual realm should remember one thing. God can do whatever He chooses and is delighted to partner with us all to accomplish His will.

This book is a peek inside my walk with God revealing how the Spirit has communicated to me. He speaks to me for comfort, edification, encouragement, warnings and instructions to benefit family, friends, even strangers and me.

This book contains dozens of testimonies of how God directed my steps to reveal His loving hand in our lives. Some were led to surrender themselves to God through the prayer of salvation sometimes months before they passed away. The Spirit of God alerted me to pray for others at specific times only to hear later that their lives were in grave danger and they were miraculously rescued. You will read how God took me through a period of time where he used me to stop women from being assaulted and killed ending those men's reign of terror. My testimonies reveal God was working behind the scenes through all these encounters.

---

*Pursue love and earnestly desire spiritual gifts,
especially that you may prophecy.* (1 Corinthians 14:1)

Introduction

Stories of Hope and Victory

In one of my favorite comedy/adventure movies, City Slickers, three long-time friends took a trip to dude ranch looking for some guy fun and adventure. They were talking and decided to ask each other what was their best day and what was their worst day.

As they slowly plodded along among high cliffs of the southwestern desert, one character asked the other, "What was the best day of your life?"

It was Billy's turn who didn't want to speak. Reluctantly, Billy finally told the other two of a day when he was fourteen. He confronted his abusive and cheating father and demanded his father to leave stating he would take care of his mother and sister. The father raised his hand to hit him, but Billy never budged. Billy sadly stated that his father did leave and never bothered them again. He did take care of his mother and sister from then on ending his story with, "That was my best day!"

The next question was, "What was the worst day of your life?"

Without hesitation, Billy quickly replied, "Same day."

That well-written and unexpected moment was thought provoking and very sad. This cowboy hit the nail on the head as great things can come out of the firestorms of life. Though difficult, they can teach us the lessons God has for us if we pay attention.

As I reviewed my testimonies, I realize most of them are filled with hard times and great lessons. After all, I only rededicated my life to Jesus as an adult because I was at one of the lowest points of my life.

You will see how the Spirit uses my gifts to help my family, friends and even strangers by saving lives, bringing others to salvation by revealing the power of God's love for us all. These stories range from the thrilling and dangerous to the heartwarming.

Table of Contents

Section One:

God to the Rescue

But Christ has blessed you with the Holy Spirit. Now the Spirit stays in you and you don't need any teachers. The Spirit is truthful and teaches you everything. So stay one in your heart with Christ, as the Spirit has taught you to do, children of God. (1 John 2:27 CEV)

-1-

The Rescues

THE PITCH

The park was a flurry of activity that summer day. The little league baseball field was one of many sprawled out with a rusting chain link fence running along its perimeter. Many family members and friends cheered and whistled in encouragement for their youngsters. Most were sitting in the hot sun on the warped, dented bleachers corroded by the elements. Kids were laughing and squealing in the background. The smell of freshly mowed grass wafted through the air occasionally mixed with the tantalizing smells of concession stand hot dogs and popcorn. Off in the far distance, another crowd of spectators stood up and could be heard cheering for their team with excited hollering and clapping.

The pitcher's mound felt solid beneath his feet as he shifted his posture slightly. He dragged his cleats across it scuffing the dirt of its off-white surface finding that comfortable stance. Getting his head in the baseball game he took a moment to balance himself physically for the action ahead. He paused with the ball in his hand and glove together in front of him as he prepared his pitch.

His Vision

During his few second pause, the Spirit of the Lord showed him what was to come. All he could see was the vision set before him as all else was blacked out. He instantly recognized this as a closed vision from God as he had a lifetime of hearing similar testimonies.

In this vision, his vantage point was from about fifteen feet behind himself to his right. He watched as he witnessed himself pitch that perfect ball. He threw it fast and straight over home plate where the batter swung sending it straight back to the pitcher's mound. The vision stopped after the ball was a few feet in front of his face aimed right between his eyes. This young man had complete understanding as he recognized this vision as a warning from God and he was grateful.

Flawless Pitch

Being warned, he had more than a hunch he would execute his next pitch flawlessly. He knew his pitch and somewhat odd catch might appear eerie to the fans in the crowd. This added to his excitement. He bit back a smile. Taking aim he threw the ball hard and straight making that same perfect pitch as in the vision.

He hurled it straight and fast over home plate where the batter swung connecting with the speeding ball. The crack of the bat echoed through the park. This perfect swing sent the ball speeding straight back to him.

He immediately pulled his gloved hand up eighteen inches in front of his face. The palm of the glove between his eyes blocked his view of the batter at home plate. He stood completely still.

The baseball hurtled through the air closing the distance to him with lightning speed aimed right between his eyes. The ball landed perfectly in the waiting palm of his well worn glove. It smacked hard hitting his glove pushing it toward him a few inches. His gentle squeeze kept the ball in place.

A great hush fell over the crowd. The whole pitch and catch took merely seconds, but it thrilled this young man as God saved him from extreme injury. He knew full well under normal circumstances this line drive that zeroed in between his eyes could have been dangerous. He said a thank you for the supernatural rescue giving God all the glory.

He heard the ump yell, "Out!"

The young man grinned big with such satisfaction as he surveyed the crowd.

His mother, Natalie, was stunned by this unexpected catch. She quickly stood up as everyone looked around in confusion. She was shaken to her core at the realization her son could have been seriously injured. Catching his gaze for a few moments, she shrugged with her hands up in a questioning manner as a puzzled look ran across her face. Her mind was still racing looking for an answer to what she witnessed. She was grateful to God for her son's safety. Under her breath she whispered a thank you knowing God was at work.

All eyes were on him in astonishment as they wondered how he made that supernatural play. He knows he has seen God's mighty hand in his life having a testimony of his own. His eyes sparkled and gleamed as he beamed inside knowing he and God communicated.

My grandson, Titus, was twelve-years-old as he shared this testimony of faith in God with me. My mouth fell open and my heart raced with such joy that Titus saw a vision and recognized it as a warning from the Lord!

THE TUMBLE

My grandmother paused for a moment on the front porch. The scrap of paper that held her friend's name and address on it was in her purse. Frantically digging, she fumbled anxiously to retrieve it, so she and her friend, Mary, could visit their new friend that afternoon. She anticipated this visit all week, but she was in a hurry as usual.

Mary waited outside in the car and neither wanted to be late for their lunch date. Hurriedly, she kept glancing at Mary still searching for the address.

Upon taking her first step toward the stairs, she claimed she felt two hands push hard on the back of her shoulders. Losing her balance, she fell hard and head first down the steps. Cringing, she tensed her muscles in terror. The fall happened in slow motion as she tumbled head over heels toward the bottom stair. She had no time to extend her hands to soften the blow as one hand was inside the purse and the other was wrapped around her purse straps. She held onto hope she wouldn't break anything.

Mary jumped out of the car to offer help as she witnessed her friend begin to fall. Grandma sat crumpled on the walkway at the bottom of the stairs as her eyes bulged in a confused daze as she took stock of herself. Moving slowly at first, she felt dizzy as she sat thinking of the worst possible outcome. Silently, she and Mary's eyes met in astonishment exchanging questioning stares over the unexplainable incident they both witnessed.

Still shaken, the reality of this situation slowly sank in. She was perfectly fine. Her friend had watched the whole incident from her car and neither of them could make sense of the situation. Mary agreed with her that she tumbled two feet in the air above all eight cement stairs.

God's angels softened her fall and saved her from harm. My Grandma didn't understand and always found this incident frightening to think about as she had no explanation. She was worried the devil was going to come back and attack her again.

I was sorry she didn't see God's powerful and loving hand in her life. We spoke of this incident, but I couldn't convince her that God spared her from tragedy that afternoon.

> *For He will command His angels concerning*
> *you to guard you in all your ways.* (Psalms 91:11)

Speaking from experience as someone with the prophetic and seer gifts, I have seen these same spiritual gifts in my grandmother, mother, daughters and grandchildren. I believe the prophetic and seer gifts are God given, taught and/or caught as is evidenced in my family and friends. I've seen this form of communication between the Lord and His children activated or understood after solid explanation, examples and sound scripture.

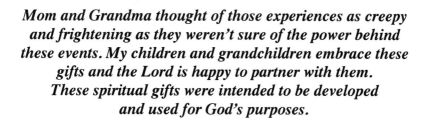

Mom and Grandma thought of those experiences as creepy and frightening as they weren't sure of the power behind these events. My children and grandchildren embrace these gifts and the Lord is happy to partner with them. These spiritual gifts were intended to be developed and used for God's purposes.

And it shall come to pass afterward, that I will pour out my Spirit on all flesh; your sons and daughters shall prophesy, your old men shall dream dreams and your young men shall see visions.
(Joel 2:28)

Ask Yourself...

- *Have unexplained incidents happened in my past?*
- *Did I immediately recognize it was God's hand in my life?*
- *What did I think at the time?*
- *What do I think now after reading these testimonies?*
- *Have I thanked God for helping me or saving me?*

2

WOUNDED PROPHET SYNDROME

I gave my life to Jesus in the 1950s at the Methodist Church in Stone Ridge, New York two months before I had my fifth birthday. I received my gifts from God at that same time. When walking under the direction of the Spirit, I am given instructions on what to do, where to go and what to say.

When the Spirit of truth comes, he will guide you into all truth.
He will not speak on his own, but will tell you what he has heard.
He will tell you about the future. (John 16:13)

Shortly after I surrendered my life to Jesus through a prayer of salvation, I saw my first vision. It was frightening, but I knew I needed to take action and God was with me to make sure my little sister would be safe.

Hearing the Holy Spirit or seeing His visions, I always knew God would be pleased at our successful outcome as He backed my every move. Fulfilling God's plans were sometimes scary, but many times they were exciting and mysterious adventures. I always knew the Lord and I would win and all I had to do was follow His directions and take that first step.

First Vision from the Spirit

Mom, my little sister, my big brother, Frank, and I were hanging out in the backyard. Nothing too interesting was going on.

As I laid face down on the warm gravel of the driveway around the corner of the house, I rested my chin on my hand. Lost in my thoughts, my attention was drawn to the fascinating plant life. I was examining these tiny Christmas tree plants with yellow balls growing between the rocks in the driveway. I wanted to leave them undisturbed and lightly touched them with my finger. I thought these plants were amazing!

My sister was interested in an object she held in her hands. With her head down, she sat on the green painted, metal well cover in the backyard. Mom was pulling weeds at the far end of the huge yard.

The Spirit alerted me by a one-second vision that zipped through my mind that my little sister was in danger. God showed me our pet rooster was about to attack, pecking and permanently blinding her right eye.

Jumping up and turning around, I rushed around the corner of the house as fast as possible. I watched as our pet rooster raced and hopped up on the well cover next to her. The rooster took a second to squat down and peer up into her face. Still racing to help, the Spirit gave me a strong feeling that the rooster was about to peck at her eye. Not able to reach her in time, I yelled her name and she lifted her head up in response. It was God's perfect timing as it pecked her cheek instead.

The rooster began flapping its wings, holding on to her and pecking in a rage, so I pulled it off and threw the rooster into the yard. Our older brother, Frank, ran over to help as the rooster came right back at her. My poor little sister screamed and flailed wildly as the rooster continued its attack, but only pecked her a few times. Frank and I kicked it away until Mom grabbed it.

After things settled down, Mom thanked me for helping my sister. I had instinctively recognized this vision as a warning for my sister and I didn't question if it was from God. I simply knew. Telling her I saw this situation before it happened in a vision from God, her head jerked back in surprise. Mom leaned down to my level and openly shamed me while shaking her finger in my face. She thought she caught me in a lie. The truth is, Mom simply didn't understand the undeveloped gifts she had were mine too, but I understood it was our loving Lord's hand in our lives.

Thinking about my statement for another moment, her face dropped. She had a frightened and eerie expression refusing to hear anymore of my story or talk to me. Mom turned and swiftly walked away only taking a brief glimpse back at me.

I suspected she became worried that I was emotionally unstable or she recognized this as an unexplained mysterious happening similar to those she experienced in her own past. Unfortunately, Mom walked away with a strange feeling with no understanding of God's protection in our lives.

My five-year-old heart moaned in anguish. My shoulders slumped and my chin trembled. I sniffed and wiped my eyes with my hand. Hoping not to appear more foolish, I took a deep breath and walked away in silence, hurt and misunderstood.

That started my long and lonely journey of living a secret life as the most cherished part of me remained hidden. The stakes were high regarding sharing with others about what God speaks to me.

The Spirit prompted me to do His bidding and I was happy to work with Him. Somewhere in the darkness of my isolation, I became the odd one and not believed. I'd most often get a scowl and the accompanying comment of, "You're weird!"

This happened in the late 1950s when such things as God speaking to us weren't spoken of or believed in our family. That summer, Mom forbid me from repeating what God spoke or showed me as it disturbed her too much.

My Mission

My mission is to share these gifts through my testimonies. It is my hope some will pray and ask for their seer and prophetic gifts too. There are others who possess these wonderful gifts questioning themselves how they always knew things, but not recognizing it was God's power in their lives all along.

I am always open and willing to partner with God doing whatever He asks of me to accomplish His plan. I can't control when or what I hear as it is always on God's timing.

God hopes to connect with us all and to understand the seer and prophetic gifts are a great way to accomplish this by establishing a direct line of communication with Him.

Secret Life

Speaking to others of my Holy Spirit encounters similar to the rooster attacking my sister usually left me emotionally stranded between two storms. As one passed another was blowing in on the heels of the last one. I took all the scoffing to heart and became emotionally wounded. At this tender age, I couldn't comprehend why I needed to suffer by simply doing God's will.

Continuing to obey God came at a great emotional expense. If I didn't follow through then God removed my peace until I did my part.

When God's prophetic words or visions came true, the people involved immediately stared at me with a puzzled look as they didn't understand. Others were always trying to figure out how I knew something or what it all meant. Nobody ever gave me a pat on the back. The people who benefited walked away usually leaving me emotionally paralyzed and terribly hurt. They'd soon forget. Or did they?

The Bible tells us the world is not our home. It also states that above all else, we are to guard our heart. I didn't figure this out until later in life.

There are millions of people like me who suffer from something called *wounded prophet syndrome*. Some of you poor souls chose to stay isolated at home rather than go out into the world and risk getting wounded time and time again. If you aren't around other people then you can't give a word. Clever, right?

If this is you, I have three words for you, "Do it anyway!"

You are God's blessed mouthpiece in this darkened world and His heart's desire is to use your gift to bless others. You are missing your blessings as well by staying isolated.

Having gifts that differ according to the grace given us, let us use them; if prophecy, in proportion to our faith.
(Romans 12:6)

Every time I share a testimony of God it sparks a memory from the listener. I listen as they share a memory or two in their lives they didn't understand before. They had chalked it up to a coincidence or to being lucky. These are the labels people attach to divine incidents when they don't recognize it was God working behind the scenes on their behalf.

The enemy of our soul has been trying to convince the Church that the Spirit isn't speaking to God's followers anymore. Even big names in the Christian community have posted these ideas on their websites with big warnings. Believing this will keep us afraid of the seer and prophetic gifts, tying our hands to render us less effective in our walk with God….and the enemy will have won.

This was the first vision from God I received. I believed this was a normal part of everyone's life, so I jumped at the chance to tell Mom. I have to ask myself what in her life could have prepared Mom to hear her five-year-old daughter claim to communicate with God?

Those prophets were moved by the Holy Spirit, and they spoke from God. (2 Peter 1:21)

Ask Yourself…

- *Thinking back, do I remember having divine visions, dreamed dreams, had feelings deep inside me, heard the Spirit speak to me or just knew things?*
- *If so, what did I do with the information or instructions the Lord gave me?*
- *What will I do next time?*

- *Am I bold enough to follow His instructions taking that first step of faith?*
- *Do I see the value in sharing these incidences with others to build their faith and mine?*

3

Trouble with the Army

Life was not easy. It was filled with the sounds of boots hitting the ground in unison as soldiers ran in formation. He concentrated on regulating his breathing, finding that comfortable pace to complete his required run. No comforts of home. No sleeping in. Sweating and hustling in the early morning hours before daybreak. Sleep was the welcomed reward at the end of each day, but never enough. One day blended in with the next and each was always tougher than expected. Boot camp was, well, boot camp!

My big brother, Frank, is tall and thin with thick, dark hair and always open for something exciting to do. He was anxious for a little rest and relaxation from training and was granted a few days off and could easily drive home for the weekend. He couldn't wait to change from his army issues to civilian clothes and have a little fun.

Frank called me hoping that he, his buddy, my first husband and I could rustle up something fun and exciting the next day. He casually mentioned that he had already invited his buddy, Tony, to spend the weekend with us. Frank told me Tony hadn't seen snow before which gave me a great idea.

I was thrilled as I made my suggestion, "Frank, let's all go skiing tomorrow at the mountain!"

Frank and Tony made the trip to our little town in Oregon late that Friday night and stayed with Mom and Dad. They planned on reporting back to Ft. Lewis late Sunday morning making their trip short and sweet.

Early the next morning, I was jarred awake by the thought that I slept through the alarm. I glanced at the glowing red numbers which read 5:30. With less enthusiasm, I shut it off before it assaulted our ears with its annoying early morning music.

I beamed as a thought occurred to me. I was combining two of my favorite things – skiing and my big brother. I missed him and had high hopes to make our trip memorable, something we'd laugh about for years to come. I recently came to the conclusion we had to make an effort to spend time together or we might grow apart.

With a promise to find adequate ski wear for Frank and his friend, I dragged the big, tattered, brown cardboard box of ski clothes from the garage to our small living room. I planned on sifting through each item. Sitting cross-legged on the living room carpet, I opened the box.

Folded neatly on top was my beautiful ski outfit. I was quiet and reflective as just looking at my outfit revived warm feelings like an old, cherished friend. I lovingly slipped my burnt orange ski jacket over my t-shirt smoothing the wrinkles out of the sleeves. It was the early 1970s and I thought my ski outfit was the epitome of high ski fashion.

Skiing can be dangerous and I had seen many skiers fall and break bones because they were too nervous. Having the right equipment along with a moderate dose of confidence was critical in this sport. Skiing was my winter passion and I was well put together with my gear and ski outfit on the slopes. Being in my early twenties, I considered myself young, tall, athletic and I was a pretty good skier.

I carefully folded the matching bib ski pants and inserted them into my duffle bag knowing they would fit nicely over my cut off jean shorts. With a big sigh, I sat on the floor and carefully examined each item in the box as I folded and packed snow gear for the four of us.

My husband and I were avid downhill skiers and we were consumed by this sport. For years we spent most winter weekends swooshing down the pristine, snow covered ski runs of Mt. Hood.

Daydreaming of our day together, I was hoping to put our skis to good use. It was going to be a warmer day with temperatures nearing sixty degrees. The snow conditions weren't favorable for great skiing which was a guarantee for an easy day with no crowds.

We decided to arrive early in the morning hoping to get a few runs in before the weather warmed up. We could ski on the crusty ice that lay on top of the slushy snow, a result of the plunging nightly temperatures.

After it warmed up, all the snow would turn to slush which meant we'd be done skiing, but could still hike in the snow around Timberline Lodge and enjoy a great meal at its fine restaurant.

We were to meet early that Saturday morning at our house. I had packed the snow gear and snacks of individual bags of chips, sandwiches and fruit in the trunk of the car before they arrived.

We loved our brand new light blue 1973 VW Bug. Frank hadn't laid eyes on it yet and he grinned big after he arrived and saw it sitting in the driveway. Frank mentioned how much he liked our new car and he'd sure like to drive it. I turned with a grin knowing he was asking to drive that day. Waiting for his next remark about him driving, I finally flipped him the keys.

I turned to put a few more items in the car. A few seconds later, the Spirit gave me a stern warning, "Joni, you need to drive back home. If Frank drives he will be in big trouble with the Army."

Frank certainly would be upset when I told him this word of warning. My brother never understood or believed, but I felt compelled to tell the group what the Spirit spoke.

I walked back into the living room where I met the other three. With a big sigh to clear some of my apprehension, I announced to the group, "Hey, Frank, I just heard God say I need to drive back home. If you drive back then you will be in big trouble with the Army."

With a great deal of eye rolling, my brother turned his head toward me slightly glaring and shaking his head as he thought, *There she goes again!*

Do not despise prophecies. (1 Thessalonians 5:20)

Raising his eyebrows, Frank asked, "What does *that* mean, Joni?"

With a modest shrug of my shoulder I said, "How should I know, I'm only telling you what I heard!"

He shook his head in a distasteful manner as he'd done so many times before. Frank mentioned that this sounded too weird to be true. The others agreed, but they went along with the idea of me driving back home from the mountain.

The four of us piled into the sporty little car with the skis strapped on top and the snow gear in the trunk. With my brother at the wheel, we sang along to our favorite oldies radio station, talked and laughed as we drove toward the mountain for our day of skiing.

On the way up to the mountain the Spirit quietly told me, "Frank won't keep his promise to let you drive, so he'll drive the car back home. It's okay as I'm revealing Myself to him today!"

Staring out the side window, I was comforted knowing we were all safe and out of danger. I also understood there would be an incident. I shook my head slightly as this would be a memorable day for Frank and I and one in which we would never forget and talk about for years to come. My hope was we would laugh about what was to come as well.

None of us had a clue what the message meant about Frank getting into big trouble with the Army. We were all curious and I'm sure none of us let this rather odd warning stray too far from our minds that day.

The sun shone brightly as we boarded the ski lift from the lodge up to the ski run. The mountain's majestic beauty of snow-covered, craggy cliffs with sharp peaks just above the tree line almost took my breath away each and every time. That day was no different.

Frank and Tony kept snapping pictures. Enjoying the familiar sights and sounds, the wind whistled along the well packed ski runs. I listened to the familiar squeak of the chair lift as we ascended higher. Turning around, I noticed the others also had silly grins similar to mine as they enjoyed their ride and the up-close picturesque view.

Our crazy idea was to double up with Frank standing on the back of my skis holding onto my shoulders. Tony and my husband doubled up too. We all loved the challenge to see if we could ski down in the unfavorable snow conditions. It was difficult to navigate, but we had so much fun as we howled with laughter and played in the snow. When I needed to stop or turn, I'd yell at Frank to jump off the back of my skis. Frank fell each time though he kept telling me he was confident the next time he'd land on his feet.

That never happened. Frank refused to wear the ski pants I packed for him as they were too short and not very cool. Instead, he wore his cool looking jeans and they soon became completely wet and he started to get cold and a little shaky, but at least he looked good... kinda! We soon headed for the lodge to get him dried out.

We had a great day poking around the mountain. We took pictures, enjoyed the sunshine, walked around the impressive lodge and enjoyed a great meal.

At the end of our day we were packing the car again for the drive home. We stood looking from the lodge in the parking lot with several lakes perched high on top of the hills and mountains. It was breathtaking with all the green trees and snow covered mountains looking miles across all the beautiful landscape.

Frank insisted he drive the car home telling me I acted way too tired to make the drive myself. I mildly protested as I knew I'd immediately be outvoted as it wasn't customary for women to drive men in that day and age. I quickly reminded everyone what I'd heard earlier that morning. They all agreed my warning wasn't real as it was too odd to be true. It was an understandable response and I knew Frank was in for a surprise sooner than later.

My curiosity grew and a part of me wanted to see how this would play out. Being more curious than upset, I muttered loud enough for the group to hear, "Well, we'll see what happens on the way home."

I wanted a front row seat of what was to come. I sat in front with Frank as I watched and waited. I kept my mouth closed and my eyes wide open. Cruising through town we were carefree talking about the day's events. From out of nowhere a pair of headlights sweeping around a corner racing through a red light charged straight at us crushing the front of the car.

We all climbed out of the car to observe the badly damaged front end. None of us were hurt, but the teenager driving the other car reluctantly admitted he was driving wildly rushing to get to his next appointment. I silently opened the glove box to retrieve the necessary paperwork handing it to my brother and husband. Saddened, I realized the car was so new I'd never opened the glove compartment other than to place the paperwork and napkins inside. The men exchanged information as I quietly scooted to the driver's seat intent on driving the rest of the way.

The prophetic word of warning kept playing over and over in my mind. I began to suspect it was happening, but it wasn't clear how my brother was in trouble with the Army yet.

Frank sat next to me and spoke up several times telling me, "I'm so sorry! I guess it wasn't so important that I drive your car home. But I still don't know what being in the trouble with the Army means."

I sat silent as the other three talked among themselves. They agreed that none of us understood the warning and it probably wasn't true. All four of us were so tired after we arrived at my house.

Sitting on the couch, I was visiting with Frank knowing he would leave soon. He was hunched over his duffle bag kneeling on the floor. Frank started gathering his belongings. He folded his clothes and shoved them in his army duffle bag carefully taking inventory of everything he brought with him. He stopped with a jolt and turned his head my way. The truth of the situation hit him like a ton of bricks.

With regret and confusion running through his mind, Frank said, "I put my army boots in the trunk for safe keeping before we left this morning."

Laughing out loud I said, "What?"

Frank shook his head in emotional agony and a vacant stare spread across his face. I stopped laughing as I observed how serious he saw his situation. He stood up hoping we could open the trunk and retrieve his army boots.

I followed Frank around the house and watched everybody's stunned reactions as he told them about his boots being stuck in the crushed trunk. All four of us went outside to the driveway. The VW bug looked so pathetic all smashed in the front. It was designed with the trunk in the front of the car where his boots were safely waiting. Frank yanked on the handle, but it was stuck.

Frank and my husband worked late into the night. They used a tire-iron, hammers, screw drivers and whatever else they could think of to pry the trunk open. It was crushed closed and nobody could open it. I saw one of them take a hammer and give it a couple of good whacks a few times out of total frustration.

I stayed up late that evening holding the flashlight as they worked, but the trunk lid wouldn't budge. With slumping shoulders, he stood and faced me. With a flat, monotone voice, Frank humbly asked if I would bring his boots to Ft. Lewis first thing on Monday morning. I agreed.

Monday morning we went to an auto body shop and they popped it right open. Mom and I drove his army boots two hours north to deliver them to Frank. He was very thankful!

In case you were wondering, he did get in big trouble with the Army. Frank's punishment was to use a toothbrush to scrub the caulking at the base of all the toilets from a kneeling position. He said it took four hours of his time after an exhausting day and wasn't such a fun job.

Again, the prophetic word from the Spirit of the Lord came true. I laughed with joy as the Lord revealed Himself to my brother again through this experience. My hope had always been that Frank would see the hand of God in his life and believe.

The Bible speaks of spiritual wisdom that is not of man, but of God. He doesn't want our faith to rest on human wisdom. He gives us words of wisdom veiled in mystery as a demonstration of the power of the Spirit.

Wanting to reveal Himself to Frank brought about a greater understanding of the Lord's ways. Frank recognized this as compelling evidence of God and Frank paid attention that day!

I knew better than to keep this prophetic word to myself. Learning early in life that if I didn't follow the Spirit's promptings, the Lord would take away my peace. This is worse than suffering through the ridicule from others after I spoke. I have the faith to always follow through after God urges me to say or do something. Most of the time it's so much fun and exciting to see the end results which rarely turns out how I imagined!

For the Lord God does nothing without
revealing secrets to His servants the prophets. (Amos 3:7)

Ask Yourself...

- *Have I had an experience where God revealed something important to me?*
- *What did I do with the information?*
- *What was the circumstance and what was my response?*
- *Has my view on this subject changed over time?*
- *How has it changed and why?*

-4-

Grizzly Adventure

I tugged at my sweatshirt to straighten it as I carefully squared my shoulders. Stretching my arms out to keep my balance, I cautiously stood up. Finishing my difficult climb of about 25 feet, I felt satisfied. I stood atop several large boulders that were perched high over a cliff close to a graveled area off the main road. I stood still as I scanned the scenery before me.

The view was breathtaking. I shook my head at the realization that I had driven by Yellowstone numerous times. Being a single woman in her late forties, it was about time I stopped.

I was an observer of what appeared to be a new Disney theme park of Mars. The diverse landscape in Yellowstone National Park seemed like two million acres of oddities. Everywhere I turned was the beautiful creation of the violent aftermath of volcanoes many thousands of years ago. Standing tall on top of the world, I could see many miles in every direction.

The rock formations below me appeared to be straight from another planet. The landscape seemed artificial, sculpted by a special effects team rather than by geologic forces. Its vast valleys were made from volcanic rocks of all sizes and were filled with geysers, hot springs, cliffs, mountains, lakes and streams.

Puffs of steam were billowing high in the air. I saw wooden walkways built to entice an interested viewer to take a closer look at the eerie, glistening ponds which occasionally burped up through the sludge.

It was just before ten o'clock that morning and I came upon a long, straight, stretch of paved road at the bottom of a valley floor with high hills on both sides. Those steep hills were mostly barren, but dotted with a few bushes, brown grass and scrub trees growing in clumps.

I shielded my eyes with my hand, straining to discern the movement at the top of the hill to my right. I saw a large, brown dot and two smaller ones moving at a fairly rapid pace down the hill from my right. A mama Grizzly bear and two cubs were coming my way! In my one day visit to Yellowstone I was hoping to see a Grizzly bear or two in the wild and there they were giving me my own private showing!

I stopped in the middle of my lane and turned the car off. Not wanting to scare her away, I didn't pick up my camera for pictures. I watched in amusement for five minutes as the cubs playfully jumped and chased each other then ran to catch up with their mama. All three bears ran down the hill and actually ended up about twenty feet directly in front of my car.

I said to myself, *Wow, what a blessing!* The mama stopped in the middle of the road in front of my car. She stood waiting as her two cubs ran halfway up the hill to my left. She seemed oblivious to me as she didn't even give me a sideways glance. I chuckled to myself thinking that I might have appeared to be a red rock to her which was the color of my car. Then I grinned, wondering if bears are color blind. *It didn't matter*, I thought, *I'm safely tucked away in my car*.

Her babies were half way up the other huge hill to my left with the mama bear watching carefully. My attention went from the cubs to the mama bear.

Suddenly, she stood up and walked toward my car. She opened her mouth and shook her head baring her teeth and claws. My head jerked back abruptly at this unforeseen turn of events as I understood the mama bear was waiting for her cubs to get far enough up the hill to safety before dealing with me. I had invaded her territory and she viewed me as an unwanted intruder.

In that moment, I realized she was angry at me because I had trespassed in her backyard where she had been raising her cubs. The

Grizzly growled long and hard and gave me ample warning to stay away from her cubs. I was petrified!

She had her claws up and I watched as she closed the distance to my car. She was only a few feet from the front of my car when our eyes locked. Grizzly bears take it as an act of aggression if you stare directly into their eyes. I knew that to be a fact, but I still couldn't avert my eyes as I was frozen in terror!

Time stood still for a moment as my mind was shutting down in fear. Inside my head, I was screaming, but on the outside I sat gasping for air.

The reality of Grizzly bears seemed to catch up to me with all the frightening stories I'd heard and read. Stories flooded my mind about how these mighty beasts can use their powerful claws to peel car doors off their hinges in short order. Well, so I've heard. A single swipe with their mighty paw could break a window and they could tear into the interior of a car and its occupants if these huge beasts so desired.

Suddenly, I realized I was not safely tucked away in my car, but helplessly trapped in my tin can of a car! I knew this scene could turn ugly and I was faced with an angry mama Grizzly bear.

I had to think fast! I faintly whispered, "Jesus, help me!" I was afraid to move or be too loud. In a split second, all these thoughts seemed to run through my mind simultaneously. *How fast could I turn the car on and start driving backwards? Was I going to die or worse; would she maul me and leave me in a heap on the side of the road?*

She took a few steps closer and her belly almost touched the front of my car. Her huge frame seemed to have filled up two thirds of my windshield as I realized she wasn't an inferior beast at all, but a protective mother.

Suspended somewhere between being a visitor and a victim of my current and unforgiving circumstances, I hoped the Grizzly bear didn't want to take it a step further by ending my life. I wanted to live.

She stopped growling and gave one last breathy grunt as she fell down hard on all fours again. It was frightening to hear her heavy paws land on the ground with such a solid thud that I felt it from my car. It took this Grizzly less than a minute to catch up with her cubs and all three of them became little dots again as they were halfway up the hill. I had no idea she could run that fast. She went merrily on her way up the hill with the two cubs playfully running and jumping on one another. I'm sure she forgot all about me moments after this encounter, but I'll never forget her!

I immediately turned the car on and drove as fast as I dared straight ahead resisting the urge to speed. I shook with fear headed for the next exit as I was done with Yellowstone. This place had turned into a nightmare!

I did call out to God for help, but I couldn't call it a prayer though God still heard my plea. Relieved I survived this encounter, it could have been much worse. It was then I remembered I had not prayed that morning.

Seek the Lord and His strength; seek His presence continually.
(1 Chronicles 16:11)

Driving toward the exit, I connected to God through love, praying with a thankful heart that I was still alive. Within a minute, I was feeling confident and surprised at how easy it was to go from trembling terror to such godly peace in His presence.

A little over an hour had gone by and I was having a great time still connected to God through praising, praying and music. I was fairly confident that I was headed in the right direction toward the exit. I was reveling in all the sights I stumbled upon during the final leg of my trip.

———————⋙⋘———————

I admit that my heart wasn't set on the Lord that morning, but on my trip and myself. I was too busy for God and had forgotten Him that morning, but the Lord hadn't forgotten me!

The truth is that I was surrounded by angelic hosts— His armies of angels in Yellowstone. Read the following verses, commit them to memory and know that the Lord has encamped around you with his angelic armies who heed His commands to guard and protect you.

———————⋙⋘———————

*The angel of the Lord encamps around those who fear Him, and
delivers them. (Psalm 34:7)*

*He who dwells in the shelter of the most High
will rest in the shadow of the Almighty.
I will say of the Lord, "He is my refuge
and my fortress,
my God, in whom I trust."*

*For He, (the Lord), will command His angels concerning you
to guard you in all your ways;
they will lift you up in their hands,
so that you will not strike your foot against a stone.
You will tread upon the lion and the cobra;
you will trample the great lion and the serpent.*
(Psalms 91:1-2, 11-13)

Ask Yourself...

- *Have I ever found myself too busy to pray in the morning?*
- *How did that turn out for me?*
- *Can I see how the author was spared from the Grizzly by being a child of God?*
- *What will I strive to do every morning from now on?*

More Yellowstone Adventures

G od's peace resonated within me as I kept driving following the exit signs. I shook my head and chuckled as my simple one day excursion in Yellowstone was already full of unexpected adventure. And all before noon! *After all*, I thought to myself, *I got what I bargained for as I was hoping for adventure!*

I was organized with my water bottle, my open map on the passenger seat and my box of music CDs. I was settled into my minivan for a long day of driving as I headed for the highway. All was well again.

Having driven almost an hour and a half, I still wondered how far I was from the exit. Yellowstone was still awe inspiring and I'd often pull over for a quick peek at the beauty offered at each perfectly placed viewing area.

It was almost eleven thirty in the morning. The road I was driving on was curvy, so I drove slower than usual. I carefully rounded a corner and happened upon an older motor home parked about forty feet in front of me on the road. I stopped to analyze this scene as I sensed something was wrong. I could see exhaust coming from the tailpipe, so I knew the engine was running.

There were maybe a hundred bison surrounding this motor home and boxing it in while stopping the occupants from being able to drive anywhere. The bison had no immediate plans to budge as they stood around, grazing and casually taking in their surroundings.

I rolled my window down and glanced at the idling motor home. I noticed a man's left arm out the rolled down, driver's side window. I saw him beating the outside of the door with his doubled up fist in an attempt to scare the beasts away from his vehicle with the hopes of driving down the road. Obviously, it wasn't working.

I heard the Spirit direct me, "Go help them!"

"Okay!" I said out loud. I was excited! After all, how many people hear an invitation from God to walk safely among bison at Yellowstone National Park?

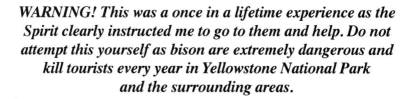

WARNING! This was a once in a lifetime experience as the Spirit clearly instructed me to go to them and help. Do not attempt this yourself as bison are extremely dangerous and kill tourists every year in Yellowstone National Park and the surrounding areas.

God understood I needed Him to confirm or deny to me that I heard correctly. The Spirit gave me a strong feeling deep inside, directing me to walk among the dangerous bison. I had God's peace and confidence as I was already primed and ready to be used through all the praising and prayers over the last hour and a half. I was in for a big adventure to help whoever was trapped in their motor home while not knowing what kind of help they needed.

I parked my car and took a few steps toward the herd. A wave of God's love washed over me and I sensed the immense love God had for the trapped people and He wanted them safe. Walking in the anointing of God, I loved them too. I felt such peace and contentment.

Walking Among Bison

My heart was bursting with excitement at my current assignment. There were no other cars ahead or behind us, but that was soon to change. Without hesitation, I started my trek toward the herd with confidence in God. I knew the bison were dirty and I thought about quickly changing into my long pants. But no, I felt the Lord compel me to stroll toward the motor home.

In an attempt to help me, I heard a man scream from a long distance away, "Get back to your car, you're not safe!"

I was on a mission and couldn't delay, so I turned back with a reluctant wave and a half-hearted smirk.

An attractive couple in a small, dark car parked behind me. The woman shook her head as she shielded her eyes with her hand positioning her head downward. She didn't want to view the gruesome sight of what was sure to come, but curiosity moved her and she glanced up often to take a few quick peeks. As she turned away, I'm sure she shuddered as her mind kept wandering to the nightmarish scene being played out before her. She sat helplessly with a front row seat not being able to turn away.

The young man beside her feverishly scrambled to get his camera out. He had a nervous smile on his face. They both expected the scene to turn grisly any second and he wanted it all on film. She wanted no part of this emotional trauma. We glanced at each other for an instant as her eyes pleaded and begged me to stop and turn around toward safety.

I shrugged my shoulders at her with sorrow and trudged forward. I had no qualms as I trekked through the herd, but I felt sorry for the pitiful spectators who were surely terrified by my bizarre actions. I shook my head at this odd situation knowing that if I told someone I was on a mission from God then I'd appear even more crazy. The Spirit urged me to walk onward to help those helpless people stuck in their motor home.

Within a few seconds, more cars stacked up and people piled out staring at this alarming scene while heckling me. I hesitated and did an about face to give them a couple of good photo shots of me as I smiled and waved. I chuckled as I'm sure they thought these were the last few photos of me alive.

While I walked in the Spirit, I was excited and fearless as I continued forward. The majestic beasts were covered in long, feathery, brown and black fur. It was spring and it appeared as if the bison were shedding their fur in large clumps, but they stood undisturbed by me as I walked among them. Their backs stood maybe five feet tall. I am a tall woman, so I walked through the herd with my arms up above shoulder height as I bent my elbows as if wading through water not wanting to get my arms wet. I walked through them slowly as they stood close to one another as the sides of their bellies touched each other.

As I approached two of the bison, I walked between their heads and touched their bony spines as if giving a gentle order to move aside. This amused me as the fur on their spines twitched wildly left and right for a few seconds. These wild animals were held at bay, naturally responding to God as they stepped aside to allow me enough room to pass. I used this technique each time and slowly made my way toward the motor home.

Taking my time to examine these magnificent beasts, I didn't feel I needed to rush. I felt I had God's permission to go slowly and enjoy this once-in-a-lifetime experience.

The Rescue

Five minutes later, I arrived at the driver's window and I was shocked! The elderly man was so angry that his face, neck and head were a deep purple, shockingly accentuated by his short sleeved, white t-shirt. He didn't notice me even though I stood at his window four feet away. This older gentleman continued to beat his left fist against the outside of the door making the dent huge.

It was obvious that he had beaten the door and waited a long time as it appeared he was lost in a trance of exhaustive anger and poor health and not doing well physically. The thought came to me that he was going to collapse if he didn't settle down soon. I peered up as he stared straight ahead banging the door with his fist.

"Are you watching the bison or do you want to get out of here?" I asked, though I knew the answer.

This was my clumsy attempt to break his trance like state of anger.

He glanced at me for a split second and said, "We've been here for an hour and a half and these bison won't budge and let us go through!"

Hmm, they'd been there an hour and a half? My first thought was that I had left the terrifying Grizzly and started to pray at the same time the man had become stuck in the bison. As I spoke, his petite wife leaned forward in the passenger seat and smiled nervously.

She appeared to be so thankful with hands pressed together in a prayer like manner as she mouthed, "Thank you."

She bowed her head ever so slightly.

I grinned at her and mouthed back, "You're welcome."

She smiled and shut her eyes as if to thank God for the rescue then leaned back into her seat and out of my sight again. I stood at his window for another minute as I tried to figure out how to calm him down, but nothing came to mind.

> *When the righteous cry out, the Lord hears and*
> *delivers them out of all their troubles.* (Psalms 34:17)

Then I said in a sharp, commanding voice, "Follow me and I'll get you outta here!"

I felt confident the man had settled down enough. I planned to wade through the bison for another five minutes to enjoy these huge animals on my way back to the car.

As I started my journey back, I became aware of the hoots and hollers from the rapidly growing crowd of hecklers. I glanced up and noticed a long line of cars parked behind mine. The boisterous crowd had grown much larger and consisted mostly of men and boys. These observers snapped pictures and filmed all that I did through jeers and laughter. I judged from their anxious conduct they were pretty nervous and were masking their fear through banter and jokes. I can't fault them for their morbid curiosity. I totally understood their reaction to this peculiar situation.

They must have been disgusted at this seemingly mindless woman wandering through such dangerous animals. They were certain I'd be gored to death any second and they wanted to capture the whole chilling scene on film.

After all, everyone knows bison don't put up with people touching them. It was just a matter of time before those animals would become angry and attack me. I knew that wasn't the case with me and for this one time in my life.

***I was following the Spirit's
instructions and walking in His will.***

Taking my time, I slowly waded back toward my car through the sea of wild animals. But these bison had the most beautiful and gentle, big, brown eyes with the longest eyelashes I'd ever seen. I was drawn to get a closer look at those perfect eyes that watched me. Remembering the eyes are the windows to the soul, I took full advantage of this profound moment.

This was my one chance as I bent over to stare one directly in its eye as I caught its gaze. I was five inches away from it and I seriously wondered if I could catch a glimpse of God or an angel as this mighty animal grazed calmly. Nope, all I saw was a big, beautiful, brown eye with gorgeous long eyelashes nonchalantly staring back at me.

We weren't particularly disturbed by each other. I thought again how those noble animals and I were obeying God's will in total harmony. Of that I was sure.

While having my picture taken, I did what any reasonably cautious, conservative, Spirit-filled Christian woman would do in such a dangerous situation. I put on a show for my captive audience! I rested the tips of my index fingers on the tops of two bison's horns as I stood between them tipping my head to the side a little to strike a confident pose. The bison carefully shook their heads slightly from side to side. I smiled and waved at the crowd.

Still at the edge of the herd, I crossed my legs at the ankles and bowed low as I made a sweeping motion with my right arm as if to say, *Thank you, it's been my pleasure!*

My final gesture before I left the herd was to put my hands in the air and shrug my shoulders as if to say *I know what you expected, but it didn't happen!* The watching crowd tried to remain calm as their minds filled with horrifying possibilities.

The Spirit instructed me through a quick, two-second vision as I walked back to my minivan. He showed me how to get the herd of bison to move far enough away from the road for us all to drive by. I made the same large, sweeping, circular motions out the window with my left arm. Driving past the herd, I poked my head out the window thanking the bison for moving aside. Again, these regal animals naturally responded to my hand gestures as was God's will.

This was such a great adventure and I fell in love with bison. I also realize this was a once-in-a-lifetime opportunity and one that the Lord will probably never ask me to repeat. I'd never take a foolish chance to walk among them again.

...and shall not fear the beasts of the earth.
...and the beasts of the field will be at peace with you. (Job 5:22-23)

I drove as if in a parade. The bison quickly shuffled off the road about thirty feet away which gave us more than enough room to drive through. The motor home and all the rest of the cars followed behind me and formed a caravan making our way down the road.

As I led the caravan, I stopped for a second and took a picture of a few bison and the motor home. It's not a particularly good picture and seems a little insignificant, but it's all I have of the memory.

———◦◦⊂⋙⊃◦◦———

WARNING! This was a once in a lifetime experience as the Spirit clearly instructed me to go to them and help. I would never attempt to do this again. Do not attempt this yourself as bison are extremely dangerous and kill tourists every year in Yellowstone National Park and the surrounding areas.

———◦◦⊂⋙⊃◦◦———

Grizzly Versus Bison

What was the difference between the frightening Grizzly and the fun bison experience? I wonder if it was a matter of not having prayed that morning, but still being protected as a child of God.

After the Grizzly experience, I prayed with all my heart, grateful that I hadn't been attacked. The frightening Grizzly episode was what lit the fire under me to connect fully with God through prayer and praise.

God wanted me to experience the difference between no prayer and praying fully engaged with my whole heart. I prefer to live my life fully engaged with Jesus. I'll not only be protected from the Grizzly, or should I say grisly circumstances of life, but also have fun adventures like walking peacefully among the beasts of the field with the Lord's blessings!

God's answer for the praying wife on behalf of her ailing husband might have been my answer to a fun adventure in Yellowstone National Park. Do you suppose God matched my praising Him with all my heart and her heartfelt prayers to rescue her ailing husband?

Whenever I hear the Spirit ask me to take action on His behalf, I know I am activating and releasing the supernatural realm by taking that first step in faith. The Spirit is always with me and my mission is usually obvious fairly soon, but not always.

Call upon me in the day of trouble; I will deliver you, and you shall glorify me. (Psalms 50:15)

Ask Yourself...

- *Have I clearly seen the difference it makes when I pray in the morning with a grateful heart?*
- *Do I want to be available to God and work for Him?*
- *Can I see the difference after the author spent time with God praising and worshipping, then Him asking her to walk among the bison to save the couple in the motor home?*
- *Do I think the wife recognized that God answered her prayer for her ailing husband by the author's help?*
- *What do you think of the author's conclusion?*

-6-

Forked Stick

I had a moment of clarity just before my first step into the herd. The Lord revived a memory from decades earlier that seemed to bring peace about my hike through the bison.

This memory began when I was driving my car headed toward our farm in Yamhill, Oregon with my big brother, Frank, and our cousin, Jeff, who was riding in the back seat. Jeff wanted to see our property and house which was still under construction.

As we rounded the corner a half mile from our house, I saw our eighty head of cattle had escaped and were slowly grazing along the side of the road headed in our direction. We stopped and climbed out of the car. As we were standing twenty feet in front of them, they stopped and stood. Not one of them chewed once as they froze in their tracks and intensely observed us waiting for our next move. They knew they were going back to the field, but were waiting for my first move.

We were in our twenties at the time and both men were well over six feet tall and in great shape. I asked Frank and Jeff to help me herd them back. I told them we could walk up to them and clap our hands a few times and watch them turn around and head for the field. They both apologized and admitted that they were afraid of the cows and the few steers. They were both sorry, but refused to help stating they didn't want to get hurt.

Needing their help, I had to think quickly as I wasn't sure I could do it alone as the cattle might walk right past our driveway.

I saw a stick shaped in a perfect "Y" and told them cows are afraid of forked sticks. As a joke, I explained that if they held these sticks out in front of the cows they'd turn around and hurry back home.

Never being able to trick either Frank or Jeff, I handed Jeff the stick and he stuck it out and took a small, cautious step toward the wayward beasts. The whole herd immediately turned around and headed back to the field in a hurry. Jeff glanced back at me nodding with a sense of confidence and awe as he smiled. Wanting to bend over in laughter that I finally tricked my cousin, I nodded and raised my eyebrows, smiling back as if to say, *See, I told you it would work!*

Frank's no dummy! When he realized the great success Jeff was having with the forked stick, he agreed to help. He slowly drove past the herd to park just after the entrance to the driveway. The plan was that the cows would simply run up the driveway and into the field where they escaped.

Jeff and I walked behind and herded them back to the field. I could only glance at Jeff one time as I didn't want to burst out laughing. He held the forked stick as far out in front of him as he could. He had sufficient confidence walking next to me, but I noticed his head tilted back and to the side as he peeked forward from one eye as an added safety precaution to keep a healthy distance from the cows.

We came closer to the driveway where Frank leaned against my car grinning proudly. The herd turned in and walked back into the fenced area. I turned to look at Frank and I lost my composure when I noticed his huge forked branch he must have found in the ditch at the end of his extended arm too. Frank seemed so silly with all his confidence in that powerless tree limb. I leaned over with a huge burst of uncontrollable laughter while Frank and Jeff instantly recognized I tricked them!

In Yellowstone National Park, I was a little nervous to begin my hike through the dangerous bison. God reminded me of that fun memory and used it to bring me comfort and give me confidence. The Spirit gave me a strong idea to treat the bison like the herd of cows as I had so many years before. Realizing I had God's protection over my actions, I felt protected to walk through the herd of bison to help the trapped people in the motor home. Before my first step, I bent over laughing and knew God did too at that old memory much like any two people do in a relationship.

———⊙⊂⊱⊰⊃⊙———

I chuckled when the Lord revived this fun, old memory of Frank and Jeff to my mind seconds before I entered the herd of bison. All apprehension for my current assignment seemed to evaporate as I viewed them as that herd of cows. I fully understood I didn't need a flimsy forked stick for protection as I have God almighty in my life.

The Lord went before me to smooth out my path in the spiritual realm so my walking in the physical realm became flawless.

Jeff may have been tricked, but he and his wife know who to call on in times of trouble. He and his lovely wife have dedicated their lives as pastors to spread the good news of Jesus Christ and have taught me so much!

———⊙⊂⊱⊰⊃⊙———

Commit your works to the Lord, and your thoughts will be established. (Proverbs 16:3)

Ask Yourself...

- *Can I see the author was given a dangerous assignment and God immediately gave her the tools to find the peace she needed to be successful?*
- *Do I want a close enough relationship with God that I expect His help when needed?*
- *What steps do I need to take for this to happen in my life too?*

-7-

Shattered Dreams

O ur howls of laughter echoed through the halls of that restaurant during our company party and awards ceremony. I was a medical transcriptionist. I had just received my Cow Pie award in recognition for all of my hard work, an award represented by the coffee cup that sat in front of me. All nine of us were enjoying our business meeting at a Mexican restaurant an hour from my home.

These words were beautifully inscribed across the outside of my mug as this is what I heard on the recording as I tried to transcribe what the doctor spoke. This doctor was known for her garbled speech into the microphone. She was not very clear in her speaking as I heard her say *cow pie* while sucking on lemon drops which rolled and clicked against her teeth as she dictated.

My children were young and I worked part-time from home. I worked when the children were at school and after they went to bed. I loved this work as it fit perfectly into my schedule.

In the middle of all the partying and laughing, the Spirit notified me that I needed to get home immediately. I had a terrible, sinking feeling that something was very wrong and I became desperate to collect my belongings and leave. In a mere second, I went from laughing to being gravely concerned and my feelings showed plainly on my face. My friend asked me what was wrong and all I could tell her was that I needed to go home. She was confused by my radical change of actions and words.

I quickly stood up and bolted for the door. I raced across the parking lot to my car headed for home trying to contain my panic, afraid of what I would find.

This was in the late 1980s, a time before cell phones existed. I prayed all the way home and tried not to speed. My three kids and their father were at home and I tried to keep my fear at bay through prayer.

I arrived an hour later and saw my three children sitting side by side on the couch, backs straight and hands folded in their laps. This scene was likely staged by their father. All three children had strange expressions on their faces and were completely silent. I knew something happened, but it was over for the time being.

Shattered Dreams

The next morning, my husband acted like all was well. He was laughing and loving to us all as he left to plow the field. Then I talked to the kids and found out things had gone from bad to worse. My heart sank as I decided never to allow this abuse to happen again. All my dreams of a happy family life seemed to crumble before my eyes.

The more I thought about it the angrier I became. I went from calm to furious in a split second. I lost control and became enraged as is typical of people with poor life skills who hold it all in only to have it all inevitably explode.

I headed to the filing cabinet and grabbed two handguns from the top drawer in the back. I hurried to the kitchen where the bullets were kept. I stood on a chair and grabbed a box of bullets from the top shelf behind the big, glass bowls as I was determined to make him pay for all the misery he put us through!

My plan was to drive down to the field where he was plowing and empty both pistols into him. As I was loading the first gun, I thought to myself, *He deserves to die! There isn't a jury in the world that would convict me!* This delusional act of strength might have profoundly ruined my life and the lives of my children. I believed everything I told myself, but they were all lies from the devil!

Hearing the Spirit

After I loaded three bullets, I heard the Spirit's calm voice speak to me loud and clear, "He'll be dead. You'll be in jail, so who will raise your children?"

The Spirit showed me the saddest vision. I saw my three beautiful children standing on the corner of the street waiting for a car to pass before they finished their walk to school. They were dressed in the finest clothes. I saw their broken hearts, their deep sadness being raised by my Mom and Dad with me rotting in jail all because of this one moment of rage.

Through my immaturity, I came to this crossroad as my emotions catapulted me from a victim mentality to rage and fury through my bitterness and anger. Being a child of God, I should have relied on Him and called out to Jesus for my help. I didn't fully understand this godly concept and had a lot to learn.

I glanced over at my children as they ate their breakfast. They were totally innocent and didn't know what I had almost done.

Expressing my gratitude to God for stopping me, I immediately unloaded the pistols and put everything away. I didn't know what to do as I was so broken and emotionally stunted. God made me realize violence was definitely not the solution. Once again, I found my strength in God alone!

I collected my thoughts and walked outside on the porch and prayed.

I spoke to God through my tears. "I don't want a divorce, but I have to consider my three children."

The Spirit spoke to me loud and clear, "You are released from the bondages of this marriage."

I continued to ask Him, "What about our future? We were planning on selling this property to pay for our retirement."

"I am your retirement. You can depend on me," He answered.

I heard a word from the Spirit years earlier about him which kept me clinging to hope all those years for our failing marriage.

I reminded God of the prophetic word as I said, "You told me he will counsel many who are like him."

Not yet fully mature in God's ways, I created a reasonable scenario in my mind and believed it. I envisioned he would successfully lead a men's group counseling other abusive men at a local church. I reminded the Lord of His specific word.

The Spirit's answer was simple and to the point. "Did I say it would be within the confines of your marriage?"

The answer was a big, fat no. Emotionally, I was just twirling in the wind with no direction when God stood beside me in grief at the loss of my marriage and the death of my dream life.

I divorced my husband. So many times I would be frustrated by my predicament. At these low times, I would crumble emotionally wherever I was and cry. Crying and having big pity parties was all I knew to do. Eventually, I lost friends over my constant whining and rightfully so.

In my immature mind, I thought my ex-husband was such a mean person. Every time something upsetting happened, I automatically blamed him whether or not it was his fault. I blamed him when the ladder went missing even though I found it on the other side of the house later. It was his fault when a suspicious cowboy drove up our driveway in his pick-up truck after dark. I blamed him for the buckets of tears I cried when my uncle graciously removed a dead skunk from our well water. I pointed my finger of blame at him when someone made a prank call in the middle of the night and when my car wouldn't start until I figured out it needed to be in park.

Filling my emotional tank with fear and anxiety as a victim, I gave my ex-husband total reign over my emotions. I was not living the abundant life, but playing into the devil's hand. Needing God's help, I prayed.

God's boot camp isn't easy, but is always the best avenue. These times were some of the worst and the best. God can pick up the broken pieces of our lives and transform us into the likeness of Jesus if we will open up to Him.

I believed the lies of the enemy as I thought I was being strong and brave. The Spirit spoke to me and it became clear that I behaved foolishly and recklessly. I am so grateful the Lord stopped me, saving not only myself, but for protecting the future of my three innocent children.

I heard the Spirit and we all averted tragedy that morning. My whole family was spared from life-changing suffering because the Spirit calmly explained what my children's future would have become if I allowed my emotions to rule over me.

Not only did the devil lose, but God gets all the glory for that huge victory. I have the pleasure to pass along what I've learned!

Because I listened to the voice of the Spirit, the lives of my children were instead filled with a life of God's favor, promises, opportunities, personal growth, travel, education, God's wisdom, love and happiness. Mine was too!
Thank you, Jesus.

Haven't I commanded you? Be strong and courageous. Do not be frightened or dismayed, for the Lord your God is with you wherever you go. (Joshua 1:9)

Ask Yourself…

- *Am I allowing someone or something to steal my peace?*
- *Am I filled with fear and anxiety?*
- *Who do I need to turn to in these times of emotional confusion?*
- *Am I aware that I can simply call out to Jesus and ask Him to help me?*

-8-

Prophecy Realized

Twenty years later, my husband, Bernie, and my son, Duane, monitored my health as my strength faded and exhaustion overtook me. Within a few days, my illness, had progressed to pneumonia. As a former firefighter, I recognized the symptoms of the high fever as I wheezed, coughed and suffered with labored breathing. In my weakened state I was unable to get out of bed, shower, or eat much of anything for a total of eight days.

God was in control and I refused to let my faith waiver. During my illness, I couldn't comprehend why the Spirit directed me not to go to the doctor or the hospital. Concerned for my failing health, Duane told his dad about my pneumonia.

The next morning my ex-husband knocked on the front door of our house. He dashed back down the six steps of the porch as he felt like a stranger and unsure if he would be warmly greeted or bitterly turned away. Bernie opened the door and was taken aback to see him as he stood off the porch. He nervously toted a large bottle of silver in both of his hands. Bernie could see by his attitude he was very anxious about being at our house, but Bernie greeted him and invited our guest inside.

He refused the invitation, but instead raised the bottle as a gesture of friendship as an offer to help as he gingerly climbed each step. He explained his natural health care modality and was confident it would take care of my pneumonia. He continued to offer information on how often each dose should be taken. He handed the bottle to Bernie, turned around and headed back to his car.

Bernie offered me the bottle and explained the dosage and on day five I would be well again. I took my ex-husband's advice and the next morning I did feel about twenty percent better. I took my first shower.

I wanted verification of my pneumonia, so I made an appointment with my doctor. She provided the diagnosis that I did have pneumonia and it was quite serious. Her professional advice was that I might die if I didn't check into the hospital right away. I had no doubts that my ex-husband's homeopathic remedy would heal the pneumonia. I had been hearing the Lord tell me not to go to the doctor for treatment and I figured this was God's reason. I followed his advice and within five days I was totally fine.

Dani, my son-in-law became ill with pneumonia a few months later. He used the same silver and was fine within five days too.

This was the start of a new relationship as Bernie started to invite my ex-husband to family get-togethers. Now we celebrate holidays and birthdays together as he's part of our immediate family. My ex-husband stated he didn't remember this incident and I understand. He has helped many others throughout the years with their health as well.

After those two miracles, the whole family started listening to what he had to say. We have all learned so much about staying healthy. I know this is the ministry that the Lord had told me about so many years before. He is counseling so many of us who are just like him, people wanting to get healthy and stay healthy through natural ways.

God was executing His glorious plan as my ex-husband followed the Spirit's subtle guidance. That brief moment on my porch so many years ago impacted our whole family. I know he didn't drive to my house on an impulse, but rather under God's direction. Whether or not he was aware of God guiding him to my house that morning, it still took a fair amount of courage on his part to offer his help. He followed the urging of the Spirit by bringing a bottle of silver to my house.

***This direct intervention by God led to my physical healing
and started the emotional healing between my ex-husband
and myself. It was the Lord's plan all along that through
my healing our whole family would become both physically
healthier and stronger as a family unit.***

*"For My thoughts are not your thoughts,
neither are your ways My ways," declares the Lord.* (Isaiah 55:8)

Ask Yourself…

- *Has someone I wasn't close to gone out of their way to bless me?*
- *Can I see it could have only been the Lord who prompted them?*
- *Can I see how the Lord multiplied that blessing to many others?*
- *What were the circumstances and did I take action?*
- *Reviewing this testimony, can I step out of my emotional comfort zone and take action next time I feel prompted by God to bless others?*

-9-

Flying with an Angel

D uring my divorce when I was in my thirties, the spirit of fear was my constant companion tainting all my decisions, coloring my feelings about life. My faith was getting stronger, but I was weak and untrained. God had a lot of work to do in me.

An acquaintance of mine was dying of cancer in the hospital. This was the first person I had ever known with cancer. Cancer was still less common in the 1980s than it is today. I knew this person wasn't saved and asked the Lord what to do.

For God has not given us a spirit of fear,
but of power, love and of a sound mind. (2 Timothy 1:7)

One night I prayed in earnest if I should go to the cancer ward and minister to dying people about Him. Actually, I was trying to cut a deal with God asking, "If I do this for You, will You grant me life long enough to raise my children?

Again, I was agreeing with the enemy of God who was doing a great job convincing me I was of such little value that I wouldn't even live very long. All I thought I could ask for was to raise my children to adulthood. This would fall under the category of my not knowing I was a *beloved child of God.*

As I slept that night, I found myself caught up in the Spirit, supernaturally flying as an angel carried me away to another time and place.

As we see in scripture, Philip baptized the Ethiopian eunuch and was transported by God to another place where he was needed.

And when they came up out of the water, the Spirit of the Lord carried Philip away, and the eunuch saw him no more, and went on his way rejoicing. (Acts 8:39)

And I know that this man – whether in the body or apart from the body I do not know, but God knows. (2 Corinthians 12:3)

Since God controlled these experiences, He was glorified as was in my case. God wanted to communicate something important to teach me a lesson and to build my faith. This event felt real as I could account for every moment using all my senses.

The angel and I were both stretched out flat with our heads raised like Superman to see what was ahead. Flying through time and space was beautiful as I saw distant stars glowing with brilliant white and muted, off white colors in dark space.

The angel, clad in flowing, white garments, flew above and just behind me to my left. I didn't dare steal a glance his way believing his heavenly power would overtake me somehow. All I had the nerve to do was glance a few times in my peripheral vision, but I never saw all of him. The angel didn't seem to care either way. Again, doubt and fear plagued me tainting my thoughts and actions.

I was intimidated and amazed as these thoughts ran through my mind, *Could this be my one chance to ask questions from an angel? I better pick my questions carefully as I might only get to ask a few.*

The angel took me back several thousand years to the Middle East where it was sunny and bright. We were slowly flying about twenty feet above the street of a small village. We flew above the heads of the villagers who were cheerfully doing their work, taking care of their children, tending to their animals and gardens and living a modest life. I could sense the spirit and the heart of these people. They learned to live in peace with joy in their daily lives. In my spirit, I observed this community walking in the blessings of the Lord clearly loving and following God.

This village was built with one very wide dirt and sand street running right through the middle. The houses were carved into the hills, one next to the other. The community pretty much lived, played and interacted with each other in this area. On the sides of the street were individual open and enclosed fire pits where the women cooked while watching the children and conducting their everyday activities as a community.

As we slowly flew, the villagers seemed to sense in their spirits the holiness of the angel. Most of them searched the sky hoping to catch a glimpse. They were delighted, but couldn't see either the angel or I. Some raised their arms and turned their faces upward with such joy.

The villagers were all abuzz about what was happening. Watching the mothers and fathers squat down to their children's level to explain what they sensed in the spiritual realm, a few of them put their hands lovingly on their children's shoulders and spoke to them explaining the best they knew as we slowly flew overhead. I noticed the villagers had a strong sense of family and community. I observed their enthusiasm as they wanted their children to be enriched by this experience too.

We flew maybe a hundred miles away to another small village. The sun still shone brightly, yet the atmosphere was different. I could see in the spiritual realm that there was a dark, unseen veil held in place over this village by the lies of the enemy. This veil kept the community in bondage to their sins. Believing they were less-than and worthless, they had little hope and knew so little about the love of God. These dysfunctional beliefs were passed down from generation to generation.

Having no peace or joy, these people were stuck in their misery. This community of people didn't understand how to change and I could sense they were unsure if they even wanted to put forth the energy for a better life with God. They were clueless as to where to start and seemed to have settled.

A few villagers noticed us, but instantly turned their attention elsewhere as they were uncomfortable with the unfamiliar godliness of the angel. These people had gotten used to the darkness and were filled with fear, anger and frustration. They seemed only to think of themselves, giving in to their selfish ways as this was the culture of this community. The angel didn't need to explain. People have spirits and so do communities and these spirits can be good or bad.

On the way back to my house, I became conscious I could ask this angel a question or two, but I was still afraid.

Finally, I found the nerve, "What should I do with the rest of my life?"

The angel's immediate response was, "Keep on doing what you are doing, but keep asking."

My mind opened to the truth that God was asking me to keep living my life and continue to ask Him for direction each day. This is exactly why we pray on a daily basis.

This angel also knew I had too much fear.

He addressed this issue by saying, "Do you know that nothing can happen to you that the Lord doesn't already know about first? This experience is for you now, but also when you are much older."

The angel took me back to my house and delivered me back into my bed. This seemed more like an experience than a dream. This event greatly impacted my life for many years.

When I woke up the next morning, the spirit of fear was gone and utterly broken in my life. I unloaded the gun I carried tucked in the back of my pants under my shirt and the one I hid under the seat of my car and eventually sold them. I stopped carrying my cordless phone with me everywhere at home even when I took the garbage out to the can. I saw everything differently from that day forward. All of my healing and attitude adjustment started with a simple prayer and a question and answered by an angel sent by God.

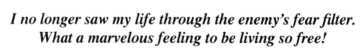

I no longer saw my life through the enemy's fear filter.
What a marvelous feeling to be living so free!

The next day I saw my ex-husband with his friend driving toward me on the driveway. As I passed by them, I didn't have any fear and didn't even roll up my window. I raised my hand casually as a sign of greeting. I nodded with a little "hello" and kept driving toward town. By the expression on his face he could tell I wasn't afraid of him anymore and his power over me was gone. I wanted to laugh as I was living in freedom.

The steps of a good man are ordered by the Lord and He delights in his way. Though he fall, he shall not be utterly cast down, for the Lord upholds him with His hand. (Psalms 37:23-24)

I hope this brings understanding and alleviates some fears in your life as well. If not, please take your concerns and fears to the Lord and He will help you. I have heard that there are 366 scriptures in the Bible that tell us not to have fear, one for each day of the year and one extra for leap year.

This important message bears repeating - before bed that night, I prayed to God, "What should I do with the rest of my life?" The angel of the Lord spoke, "Keep on doing what you are doing...but keep asking."

Knowing I had so much fear in my life, the angel also told me, "Do you know that nothing can happen to you that the Lord doesn't already know about first?"

Ask Yourself...

- *Am I allowing fear to paralyze me and keep me from doing what God desires?*
- *Do I now see the Lord will not allow me to be overwhelmed if turn to Him and ask for His direction?*
- *What lies from the enemy have I believed about myself which created bad emotional habits?*
- *Can I challenge myself to pray over those lies asking God to help me through this journey?*

-10-

God's Tool Bag

B ruce sat in his office trying to catch up on some paperwork. That anxious feeling washed over him without warning again. He briefly closed his eyes and breathed deeply. Knowing it was another one of those relentless feelings of having no peace, he knew why. Tilting his head up he scowled at himself knowing he was to blame as he lowered his chin to his chest to stretch his neck muscles and think.

He was my neighbor in Yamhill and well aware of the point the Lord was making. The Spirit had been urging him to speak to me for five days asking him to give me his valuable testimony. God took his peace away and Bruce knew what was expected of him. He could no longer ignore the Spirit's wishes.

*The things which you learned and received and heard and
saw in me, these do, and the God of peace will be with you.*
(Philippians 4:9)

Bruce leaned back in his comfy, office chair and swiveled it to face the window. He took another swig of his coffee and set it down nervously tapping his thumb against his cup. Surveying his beautiful property of gently rolling hills with tender, green sprouts of wheat blowing in the wind didn't give him his usual comfort. Beyond that was a heavily wooded forest.

Usually, he enjoyed looking out over the lush, green scenery of his property, but not that day. It was a bitterly cold and wet day in our little countryside community which was nestled in the forested hills and fields. Bruce couldn't help but notice the wind was blowing the trees. *That doesn't help,* he thought to himself as he shook his head ever so slightly. He didn't want to leave the warmth of the house on a day like that one. But not responding to God's instructions was gnawing deeply at his conscience.

He is a man's man, always planning his next hunting or fishing trip. He is a man of few words and he worked hard and had the means to give his family the best life. Bruce has a big heart and would do anything for a friend.

Bruce is also a man of God. He and his wife, Mindy, both hear the Spirit, but he wasn't ready to follow the Lord's instructions about his current assignment. It was a stretch for him and out of his comfort zone to share his testimony with me. He'd much rather hand someone a check with a grin and a handshake than to speak regarding something as intimate as how God's teaching impacted his life so radically.

And the peace of God, which surpasses all understanding,
will guard your hearts and minds through Christ Jesus.
(Philippians 4:7)

After yawning and stretching his arms, he snatched his truck keys from the dish which sat on his desk. He cut a silent deal with himself that if he saw my car parked in front of my house then he'd be obedient. As he drove down his gravel driveway, he glanced left and saw my car. He was disappointed, but he knew it was time. He drove his big truck over to my house with hesitation and asked if we could talk.

Bruce drove me to his property which adjoins ours. We sat on top of his hill overlooking my house. It was still misty as the rain hadn't stopped completely. This whole scenario was out of character for Bruce, so I knew what he had to say was important. I patiently waited with respect.

God choosing Bruce to give me this life changing message was perfect as I would always remember this one time he stepped out in faith. Mindy and I spoke daily of the Lord, so her giving me this message might not have impacted me so much. Sometimes God speaks to us through other people almost as an exclamation point so we'll remember.

Clearly, he was uneasy as he fidgeted which amused me a little at the time though my expression remained solemn.

After a minute or two of awkward chit chat, Bruce didn't hold back. He gave me his powerful testimony and his words of wisdom have been seared in my heart ever since.

Bruce told me he had been chewing tobacco for about twenty years. He tried so many times to quit, but each time he tried to beat his habit he failed. God directed him to stop chewing and Bruce knew it wasn't good for his health, but the addiction was too strong to beat.

Bruce reached down to the floor of the truck and pretended to pull up a heavy bag using both hands. He told me God gave him a bag of godly tools to use to fight his powerful addiction.

The Spirit told him to pick any tool such as praying, praising, reciting scripture, meditating on the word, listening to Christian music, singing, or anything to connect with God on a personal level when he felt the urge to chew. Every time he used one of these tools his desire for tobacco weakened.

Bruce explained that when we use God's tools, two things happen. First, in honoring God we have the help of the Lord. Secondly, the enemy flees. Every time the urge to chew became strong he would pull one of the tools out of the bag and use it immediately. He smiled and relaxed as he happily reported he was tobacco free within a few months and was done with chewing forever!

I was amazed at his testimony and how brilliant and easy the Lord made it for him to kick the addiction. Bruce had to work at his problem, but I could see how anyone could apply this same principle to any dilemma. I didn't see how using God's tool bag could help me as I didn't see how I had anything to change about myself. After I heard his testimony, I kept thinking of its simplicity and effectiveness. The Lord was trying to minister to me too.

The Spirit spoke to me about my ex-husband a few days later.

I heard, "Pray for him every time he upsets you. Every time you are tempted to cry I want you to pray. No more crying!"

That didn't sound right to me. I was a very immature Christian in my middle thirties and I questioned God's instruction. I thought,

*What? Is this for real? Are You on his side now? I thought You were
on my side? I'm the good one and he's the bad guy here! I'll do it,
but I don't want to!*

For God does not show favoritism. (Romans 2:11)

I followed God's instructions even though it all sounded too con-
tradictory and depressing just to think about praying for that wretched
man. I knew that being faithful to the Lord was all that was required
of me. My flesh was telling me the opposite, but I knew following
God was right.

God was giving me grace and mercy. It was much the same as our
earthly father would do as if holding his hands out to encourage his
giggling toddler who is thrilled to take that first step with the father
ready to catch him. The father is anxiously waiting with outstretched
arms to help soften the blow when the child falls.

The only difference was that I wasn't smiling and excited about
my new walk with God the Father. This realization that God loved
my ex-husband and me the same was a new godly concept that I
wouldn't understand for several months.

A person's wisdom yields patience.
It is to one's glory to overlook an offense. (Proverbs 19:11)

My fear was gone, but I was still angry and immature. I still
felt like the innocent victim. God had this plan to correct my immature thinking in this area as well. I heard the Spirit ask me to pray
and release it *all* to Him! I had so much pent up anger that I carried
around most of my life.

My first prayer was, "He is *Your* enemy! He is *my* enemy! Kill
him! *Kill him now!* Amen!"

It was short and to the point. I meant those awful words. I knew
I was wrong, but not sure why. I found myself huffing and puffing
a little from my anger. I realized God knew my thoughts and I was
told to release it all to Him, so I did.

Praying for this man went against my human nature, but I prayed
for him despite my negative feelings. I created this new habit and

every time I felt anger I prayed for him. Soon, I started to notice a new godly mindset. I switched over to praying for him everyday after a month simply because I wanted to pray for him.

Praying over my ex-husband was part of my journey to further heal my brokenness and deep anger. This was God's intent all along!

I wanted him to heal. My anger and despair was melting away being replaced with compassion and empathy as my heart was softening a little more each day. God was showing me a new side of prayer by maturing me more each day. I saw no difference in him, but prayer was changing me and I loved it.

So shall my word that goes out from my mouth: it will not return to me empty, without accomplishing what I desire, and without succeeding in the matter for which I sent it. (Isaiah 55:11)

About three months later, I was shown a short, open vision of my ex-husband. I was shown his brokenness and realized that I couldn't possibly harbor ill feelings against someone with such a broken heart.

A week later, the Lord showed the same open vision about me. The Lord showed me I was an emotionally stunted little four-year-old girl who yearned to have Mommy and Daddy's love, attention and appreciation. He and I were on the same playing field as I had anger and depression as well. No wonder we were attracted to each other and no wonder things went awry.

He heals the brokenhearted and binds up their wounds.
(Psalms 147:3)

Like Bruce explained, when you are upset or your heart is not in the right place, open your bag of godly tools and use whichever one you choose.

Singing Faith Over My Fear

I suddenly realized I have always used one of these tools. Even as a small child, I would sing, "Jesus Loves Me," whenever I was upset or afraid. I would start out singing almost inaudibly and within a second or two I was fine again, singing loudly without any fear. It always worked!

Now when I am combating fear, anger, depression, illness or anything troubling me, I command the situation to line up with the word of God. I can always find a few life-giving promise scriptures.

For instance, to combat illness, I couple the following scriptures and pray, "I command my body to line up with the word of God that says by Jesus' stripes I am healed. In the name of Jesus I pray. Amen!"

… declare (command) a thing, and it will be established for you…
(Job 22:28)

… By whose (Jesus') stripes you were healed. (1 Peter 2:24)

Jesus gave me the authority to cover any problem with God's powerful, life-giving scriptures. I speak what I want and not what I have as I bring life into the situation. Speaking God's word with understanding and faith is my weapon. Darkness is dispelled by the presence of light.

Occasionally, when I'm faced with a problem, confusion from the enemy will rush in and cause my thinking to be a little hazy. I look to God for help by simply speaking, "Jesus, help me." The situation will usually change immediately and I will find my answer.

As believers, we are called to be like Jesus and if we can think and speak like Him, we become more like Him. Jesus has given us the authority to do greater things than He did while on earth.

Most assuredly, I say to you, he who believes in Me, the works that I do he will do also; and greater works than these he will do because I go to My Father. And whatever you ask in My name, that I will do, that the Father may be glorified in the Son.
(John 14:12-13)

That first awful prayer regarding my ex-husband, or should I call it my desperate plea for God's help, is a great comparison to who I am today. I've learned that God doesn't play favorites as He loves us all the same. It is my personal opinion that the only difference between me and the nasty guy down the street is that I know God and maybe he doesn't yet!

Repent therefore and turn back, that your sins may be blotted out.
(Acts 3:19)

Ask Yourself…

- *Do I believe that I am called to be more like Jesus?*
- *How can I build this belief system to start behaving more like Jesus?*
- *Do I have a godly tool bag to pick from to combat fear, anger, depression or unforgiveness?*
- *Describe the process and the end results.*

Section Two:

God in the Rough Times

The next three testimonies will demonstrate how the Spirit gently guided me each step of the way to speak of Jesus to these teenagers forever changing their eternal destinies.

The fruit of the righteous is a tree of life and he who
wins souls is wise.
(Proverbs 11:30)

Gabe

"Hi everybody, I'm in the kitchen," I yelled after hearing the daily commotion by the front door of my children arriving home after school.

I heard the door open and eventually shut as the five teens bounded into our little house that Friday afternoon. They were hoping to satisfy their ravenous appetites and rustle up some fun that afternoon. I heard the sounds of several more heavy backpacks being dropped by the front door and shoes being kicked off and hitting the wall. I smiled and reminded myself to pick my battles and not let the flying shoes scraping the walls bother me while I finished wiping the counters. I heard strange voices excitedly talking and laughing from the living room.

Life was good and I had an ideal situation in the 1990's as a single mother of three. I arrived home most days in the early afternoons as I worked part time, but still made good money. I loved my children, their friends and the neighborhood kids. Wanting to keep tabs on the teens, I tried to create a welcoming atmosphere to draw them to my home. Offering food and entertainment was a great way to keep them coming back. Though I had some pretty strict rules, I hoped my house was one of their more popular hangouts.

Besides following the no shoes rule, anyone who came to our home would have to find me and greet me with a warm hello. I always knew who was in my home and we'd start each visit with respect. I expected a pleasant goodbye for the same reason. My children would always warn their friends of the rules before they arrived.

Soon, a few familiar faces strolled into the kitchen along with a few new ones. At a glance, I could see these new guests were a little rough around the edges. Being a Christian mom, I chose to see them as diamonds in the rough. I often felt God move on my heart to demonstrate His love to anyone who came to my home. That afternoon was no exception.

After the introductions and a few minutes of chit chat, I turned to the teens. "Okay, who wants pizza and a movie? It's on me! I already rented a new one and it's on top of the television. Go check it out."

Without hesitation, they all cheered. The group thanked me graciously and I nodded pleasantly at their gratitude. All I had to do was call in the pizza and make a salad. I asked everyone what they wanted on their pizzas as I ordered the most expensive and tasty pizzas in town. I could see they felt honored by this gesture.

Gabe was one of the two new, young men at our house that day. He followed me into the kitchen and helped me cut up vegetables for the salad. We talked and laughed for thirty minutes until the pizza arrived. He missed most of the movie, but kept remarking he'd rather get to know me.

Gabe remarked that he was surprised at my rules and asked me how I enforced them. I told him it was a respect issue. This young man said he hadn't met another mom like me before. Gabe suggested a few times that our house seemed peaceful and happy and he wanted to know why. Still trying to figure me out, he remarked that he could see I was a nice person. We bonded while making the salad then we set the stack of plates and silverware on the counter waiting for the pizzas to be delivered.

He asked me why I would be so kind to a group of strangers. I told him it was because we all deserve to be treated well, that we're all God's kids. He nodded his head in agreement staring off into space thinking about this new concept. He didn't understand my remark, but was intrigued noticing how comfortable I was speaking about God. He wanted to hear more, so we talked for a short time before the pizzas arrived.

This young man was tall, clever, and intelligent and I am sure he got by on his rugged good looks and winning smile. He understood how my house operated with a mix of love and discipline. We all had a fun night and I invited them all back.

He was the only one from the new group who ever came back to our house as we became friends. We developed this great mother-and-son relationship as it became evident the Spirit connected Gabe and I on a godly level.

Gabe Drawn to God

I had piqued his interest in knowing more about God. Gabe had so many questions over the next six months. Many times he watched and waited close to our house making sure I was home alone giving us ample time to privately talk more about God. He picked those times carefully, knowing he would always be welcomed in my home for our twice a month chats.

He and I shared our life stories and he loved hearing my testimonies of a loving God. His home life was not filled with love and discipline. He came from a rough family and he admitted that his parents didn't have great life skills. He simply grew up on his own. We spent many hours talking, sharing, laughing, getting to know each other, reading the Bible and praying together.

Within a few months, he made a firm commitment as his understanding of life and the Lord grew. Gabe desperately desired a godly life without all the nonsense the world had to offer. With my help, he decided to change and found good life strategies. His plan was to let go of old friends and make new ones who had the same godly values. He was a man with a plan.

Over the next six months, Gabe popped over many times. He admitted he had never heard such stories of faith and didn't know Jesus wanted a personal relationship with him. He wanted a personal relationship with Jesus too, but not quite yet.

Gabe's Incident

One rainy Friday night just before midnight, I heard a loud knock on my screen door. I woke up startled.

Grabbing my housecoat and flipping it over my shoulders, I shuffled to the front door asking, "Who is it?"

Gabe answered, "I'm so sorry, I know it's late, but I really need to talk to you right now! Something bad happened and I'm in trouble!"

I recognized his familiar voice and flipped the mail slot open with my finger as I stooped low for a peek. My daughters heard the commotion and came out of their bedrooms to check too.

So many questions ran through their minds as I spoke softly, "Please go back to bed, it's Gabe and he needs me now. We'll talk tomorrow, good night!"

They nodded and shuffled back to their rooms.

I unbolted the door for Gabe and he trudged into the living room. His shoulders were slumped in shame and remorse and he was barely able to glance my way. I saw the agony on his face that he carried in his heart. I invited him to sit on the couch. We kept quiet for the sake of my sleeping daughters then he paused with a big, uneasy sigh about the confession on his mind. My heart was breaking for my young friend who had done so well for so long. I knew it was God who drew him to my home at that late hour.

He spoke, "Something terrible happened and I'm in big trouble."

The Spirit spoke to me, "Warn him that if he broke the law and confesses, you will have to call the police on him."

I interrupted and told Gabe what the Spirit spoke to me and he readily agreed knowing it was the right course of action.

Telling me all the events from earlier that night, his fears were obvious. Tom, Gabe's friend since childhood called earlier in the evening on the phone. He was trying to persuade Gabe into joining him at a party with their old group.

Standing firm, he refused Tom's invitation of a night involving booze, drugs and rowdy behavior. His friend kept him on the phone hoping to convince Gabe through guilt and manipulation to join the party. To add more guilt, his friend said they were all hurt that Gabe didn't want to party with them anymore and they missed him terribly.

He didn't understand he had personal power to simply say no and hang up on Tom who was trying to entice him back to his old lifestyle of bad habits. Gabe admitted he became frustrated after arguing back, but finally caved in.

He had planned to leave the party early and assumed he could handle the lure of his past addictions. As the night got darker, Gabe's good intentions became weaker. Soon, he realized he wasn't up to the task and decided to leave.

He dashed out the door without so much as a quick goodbye then hurried to the bus station, so he could go home. Tom noticed Gabe's absence from the party after he heard the door slam realizing Gabe left not even a minute before. Tom ran to catch up and did so in a few minutes as they waited at the bus stop and chatted.

As Tom and Gabe boarded the bus, they were only two of eight passengers of the old, musty bus at that late hour. Each took their own bench seat and leaned their heads against the slightly vibrating, loose windows. Sitting sideways, they both stretched their legs out on the bench seats in comfort.

Gabe sighed with relief, feeling safe on the bus ride home. He closed his eyes and relaxed as he and his former friend rode toward home. He felt happy and proud he refused the offers of drugs and alcohol from his former friends. He smiled as he realized that he would never put himself in that difficult situation again. Wiser now, he understood that he could hold to his new convictions better by moving on with his life by leaving all his old friends behind.

Exhausted, he glanced at his cell phone and noticed it was only a few minutes after ten o'clock. He smiled with satisfaction realizing he had already established a new habit of going to bed early each night waking up fresh each morning ready to start the day. Shutting his eyes for a moment, he envisioned himself sleeping soundly that night, burrowing deep under the covers of his bed as his head hit the pillow.

Spending the hour together on the bus back to town the two old buddies talked. It was obvious that Tom was trying to reconnect with Gabe. They laughed and reminisced about their childhood adventures of playing baseball, swimming and bike riding. Gabe was committed that this would be their last conversation. He was anxious to restart his new life, determined never to back down again.

Tom noticed an older man on the bus and covered his mouth with his hand to muffle the details of his wicked plan. He whispered close to Gabe's ear, "Hey, Gabe, we could steal that guy's wallet after we get off the bus. I have a good plan and nobody will get hurt."

With an angry and shaky voice, Gabe responded, "What a terrible idea! That's outrageous. I don't want anything to do with your terrible plans!"

Gabe's eyes became cold as he shook his head glaring at Tom then looked away. Gabe recognized that Tom was trying to lure him back into his old, rough lifestyle. The two rode the last ten minutes in silence.

Tom lingered and allowed this elderly gentleman to step off the bus before them. Gabe exited the bus second, then Tom, third. He noticed his friend scanning the area for witnesses. Gabe recognized this behavior from past evil deeds. Gabe understood what was about to take place.

Gabe yelled a little too late saying, "Tom, noooo!"

But he was unable to stop Tom from reaching into the older man's coat pocket and roughly pull out his old, leather wallet.

Tom took off into the dark.

The older gentleman was caught off guard, lost his balance and fell to the ground. Feeling so vulnerable with utter panic on his face, he stared up into Gabe's eyes frightened, crumpled on the wet sidewalk hoping not to be further injured. Gabe had no intention of hurting anyone as it dawned on him he wasn't that person anymore. He felt sick to his stomach that someone could think of him that way.

Gabe still had poor life skills and a feeling of panic swept over him. He didn't have a solid upbringing. The family didn't have many sit down dinners together and morals were never discussed. Puzzled and frightened, he didn't know what to do or where to turn.

He hesitated in shame and remorse at the man laying helpless on the ground. This elderly man wore an old, gray wool coat and matching hat similar to what gentlemen wore thirty years before. The reality of this serious situation sank in. He turned and watched his friend disappear into the darkness with the stolen wallet containing a mere twenty dollars.

Gabe's attention was drawn to three young men who were yelling off in the distance a half block away running toward them. He wanted to help the older gentleman to his feet, but confusion settled in his mind. He ran which was his only sin.

So whoever knows the right thing to do and fails to do it,
for him it is a sin. (James 4:17)

The only thought he could wrap his mind around was to talk to me. I had been his godly friend and he hoped I had answers. He bolted as fast as he could and ran through town which was ten minutes to my house. With every slap of his foot against the wet sidewalk the dream life he worked so hard to attain faded in his mind as reality set in. His stomach churned and the old, familiar feeling of hopelessness reared its ugly head again.

Gabe decided to take a short cut to my house and run through the beautiful grounds of the local university. Turning his head, he caught a glimpse of the police station through the dimly lit stand of big trees of the university, still running until he reached my house. Gabe was caught between two worlds – the godly side was confused with his old habits of running from trouble. He confessed that he was ill prepared to correctly handle Tom's robbery and now he was going to be seen as an accomplice in the eyes of the law.

By the time he realized his running away from the scene made him an accessory to the crime, he felt it was too late. He would pay for his part in that night's event. Gabe was still an impressionable street kid and he recently celebrated his eighteenth birthday. He faced a stiff penalty as an adult.

I listened to the whole story as he tearfully gave me all the details, his heart heavy with regret. I was torn between keeping my word that I would call the police when my heart wanted to let him go free. I wanted to offer him this one free pass after we had a good talk. I had to keep my word as I heard the Spirit instruct me on what to do. I sadly told him I would make that call in fifteen minutes after we talked a little more.

I say to you that likewise there will be more joy in heaven over one sinner who repents than over ninety-nine just persons who need no repentance. (Luke 15:7)

I felt the Spirit urge me to offer Gabe the chance to give his life to Jesus through the prayer of salvation. He eagerly agreed and he meant every heartfelt word he spoke. In all his brokenness, God's peace overtook him as the blood of Jesus covered all his sins and washed him clean.

The Spirit comforted him deeply during this life changing prayer. Gabe admitted something big stirred deep in his spirit. Gabe said he became connected to God who changed this terrible moment of huge regrets into a wonderful testimony. It was clear to him that he became a different man, full of joy and understanding, desiring to seek after God.

Gabe's Arrest

When done praying and talking, I did call the police and explained that he wanted to go peacefully. I asked them to come quietly and to respect my young friend. With lights flashing, the police car drove slowly into my driveway. I hoped the police officer would be gentle and kind to Gabe as I walked out ahead and spoke with the officer for a minute.

"He has such regrets over the robbery and I am hoping for some kindness," I explained. Clarifying, I added, "Gabe just gave his life to Jesus."

That brought tears to the police officer's eyes as he nodded in agreement as indication he was a Christian too. I told the officer his kindness would demonstrate how the police can be trusted.

Thirty seconds later, Gabe came out to face the officer with a repentant heart. The officer allowed me to hug him and tell him goodbye before he asked Gabe to turn around to be handcuffed. The officer explained in a soothing voice what he could expect during the arrest then handcuffed him and gently placed him in the car to be taken to the police station. The officer turned to give me a reassuring smile while he continued to talk to Gabe in a calm manner.

Ready to burst into tears at any moment over this monumental disaster, I mouthed, "Thank you!"

He nodded in response. I was grateful as I'm sure the Lord sent that kind officer to soothe Gabe's inner turmoil as they drove to the police station.

I stood outside shivering in the cold, dark night, waving on the off chance Gabe might turn around for one last glance. He didn't. He stared straight ahead to face the consequences of his actions as a responsible man of God. A wave of sadness overtook me as I thought of this setback in Gabe's life. As the car faded in the distant fog, I choked back tears and made my way back to bed again. I prayed for everyone involved.

When I read the newspaper later that week, I found out the older man had sprained three fingers and had hurt his knee as he fell. It was understandable that the older gentleman was pretty shaken and feeling more vulnerable and unsafe to venture out of his apartment after dark. I prayed the Lord would use his trauma to bring him closer to God and he may be healed and return to his active lifestyle.

Assuming Gabe was sent to prison, I passionately prayed that he would grow closer to the Lord who would use the robbery for Gabe's good and God's glory.

Gabe's Blessings

I lost track of Gabe, but three years later I bumped into him at the local farmer's market where he had his arm around a pretty, young woman who snuggled into him. He stared at me. I stood quiet and somber, eyes brimming with tears of joy as we had this chance meeting.

He turned to the beautiful, young woman as I heard him say, "Well now, there's someone I've wanted to talk to for a long time! I'll be right back!"

Gabe's eyes welled with tears as he walked swiftly toward me with his arms stretched wide. He hugged me tight as tears fell at this heartwarming reunion.

His voice was full of love as he whispered in my ear, "The best thing for me was to go to jail. I attended a prison ministry with other believers. I've learned so much. I'm happy and serving the Lord now. Thank you for turning my life around. I'm so grateful we could catch up. I've thought about you a lot over the years."

After this terrible incident, God gently guided Gabe to run to my house where he surrendered his life to Jesus. Then the Lord placed him in a group of believers in prison who offered him the love and peace of the Lord. He grew and matured. Gabe now uses this as a testimony to bring others to Jesus. Sounds to me like God used one of Gabe's lowest points of his life as a setup and not a setback!

For I will be merciful to their unrighteousness, and their sins and their lawless deeds I will remember no more. (Hebrews 8:12)

Ask Yourself...

- *Has God ever used what I perceived as a setback as a setup for me or others?*
- *Did I do the right thing and follow through when it felt extremely difficult?*
- *Does my life show others why living for God is the right choice?*
- *Do I see that the overflow of loving God will spill out onto others?*

-12-

Scott

T he moment I waited for arrived as the waitress approached and slid the bill to the middle of the table. She centered it perfectly between Scott and me among our dirty dishes. Out of the corner of my eye, I watched as Scott picked up the bill and glanced at it. He stiffened a little and his eyes were wide open in shock from the hefty amount. I turned my head away and bit back a smile as I understood the circumstances he faced.

I've danced this dance before and knew he didn't have enough money. Young men often forget it's the multiple soft drinks and lemonades that pad the bill beyond what's in their wallet.

I discretely pulled my wallet out on my lap and grabbed two twenties. I folded them in half, caught his attention and whispered sternly for him to accept my offer. I stated that, after all, he was a kid with a part time job and I made great money. Scott pretended to argue with me for a moment as he took the responsibility of being a man very seriously.

I tucked the twenties under his plate trying not to smile.

Scott graciously thanked me. I saw his face relax again as he confidently smiled with such relief. I laughed inside and was so glad I could help him out of his predicament to save him from the embarrassment of this very common situation.

He was acting like a man and wanted to show his appreciation to us. He had invited both my daughters and I to this great restaurant that was an hour's drive away in Portland. This restaurant was his dad's favorite and he had some great times there.

Scott wanted this night to be unforgettable. My two daughters, Alicia, Natalie and I dressed up nicely for this special occasion. We did have a great meal as we spent over two hours eating, talking, laughing and sharing our lives with each other as we knew our beloved Scott well.

That memorable dinner was winding down. I was proud of who these three teens had become and loved watching their mature, relaxed interactions. The language of friendship is not spoken with words, but through actions of love.

Alicia and Scott had been dating in high school for a few years and our whole family grew to love him as they spent a lot of time at our house. Scott was a young man, handsome and sweet, so sensitive for his seventeen years.

Sharing God's Love

I was known as the preacher mom by many of my children's friends. Scott and all the other teenagers knew where I stood on most subjects. He listened to my testimonies and I tried to make him see how much God loved him too.

On many occasions, Scott would wait until I was home alone as he wanted to hear more testimonies of God. He listened to every word and he remarked often how something deep inside his spirit stirred. I considered him a valued friend and he spoke of his life with all his heartaches and great times.

His life was troubled. He didn't feel good about himself and during one of our talks he asked for help as he would give in to worldly temptations. We prayed and he did much better for a long time. Scott worked hard on reminding himself that he had a higher calling in life.

Scott told me about his hopes and dreams for his future and he wanted my advice. Most of the advice I doled out was in explaining that having a solid relationship with God would bring about blessings of a great life. God would give him the desires of his heart. After all, God put those desires in his heart.

But seek first his kingdom and his righteousness, and all these things will be given to you as well. (Matthew 6:33)

Scott's Breakthrough

Finally, Scott said he was ready to give his life to Jesus. One Saturday evening as the two of us sat alone in my house, he repeated the prayer of salvation with me. He cried and said he could sense God's Spirit knowing he was connected to God forever. From then on, he freely admitted he was a child of God and talked openly about his faith with my two daughters and me. The relationship we had with Scott seemed to open up and we all became closer to one another. I could see Scott grew in his faith, but eventually my daughter and he were no longer friends as the two teens broke up. Scott and I drifted apart and lost track of each other.

He married and had children. I heard he drifted back into his old crowd and bad habits. Our beloved Scott fought cancer for several years before he died in his early thirties. My daughters and I speak of him and miss him all these years later. We will reminisce about him until we meet again in Heaven and what a joyful time that will be!

———◦⟨✦⟩◦———

I pray asking God that Scott's children will grow up in a godly home, go to church, be fed the word and become the best versions of themselves healed and seeking the Lord. I ask the Lord to show me the results of my prayers and I believe He will.

After our beloved Scott expelled his last breath on earth he soared high with the escorting angels with eternal joy to his new home in Heaven where we'll all meet again with such joy!

———◦⟨✦⟩◦———

Jesus said to him, "I am the way, and the truth, and the life. No one comes to the Father except through me." (John 14:6)

Ask Yourself...

- *Do I step out of my comfort zone and share Jesus with those the Lord puts in my path?*
- *Can I make a bigger effort in doing so creating this new habit?*
- *Can I recognize that the author might have been the only one to step up and talk to this young man about Jesus?*
- *What are the eternal results in leading someone to Jesus?*
- *Can I be grateful that someone brought me to Jesus being bold and brave enough to do the same for others?*

-13-

Julie

M y fifteen-year-old daughter, Natalie, had taken a huge step from childhood toward becoming a responsible teen. She opened her eyes to what was happening around her. She could see the drugs, sex, rude language, rebellion, addictions and poor grades. The others joked about making a sport out of bad habits. They were hardening their hearts to all that was good and decent. Natalie could see these acts of defiance shackled them to this lifestyle. Those youths kept lowering the bar of moral depravity, trying to outdo each other in their foul behavior. She could see the brokenness, realizing their acts would lead to shame, secrets and regrets later in their young lives.

She made a firm decision that it was time to break off old relationships. She shared her high Christian standards with Julie who also decided to live a life of higher standards and they became good friends. Together, she and Julie would strive to be their very best with good grades and excellent behavior living a godly lifestyle.

Natalie told her older brother, Duane, about this big decision and he was eager to help. The two of them went shopping together and Natalie bought sophisticated clothes with sweater sets and stylish jeans. Duane jumped at his chance to help and encouraged Natalie to dress for success.

She felt great about her new commitment along with Julie. Together the girls held their heads high with confidence and spent their time studying and doing right.

Julie needed a ride home from our house after dark one evening. I offered her a ride and took Julie across our little town. On the way, she shared her life story with all the heartaches of her mom and dad's divorce. Julie cried as she told me they were involved in their new lives and she felt like an outsider. We sat in her driveway for well over an hour as I shared with her about Jesus. She loved hearing my testimonies and she could see that I'd had my troubles, but God was always there in my time of need.

Julie Turned a Corner

A strange thing happened that I have never forgotten. As we were talking in Julie's driveway that night, I opened my mouth to say what I had on my mind. Instead, what I spoke were God's words He put in my mouth.

For the Holy Spirit will teach you in that very hour what you ought to say. (Luke 12:12)

Excitedly, I spoke, "Bow your head and fold your hands. Repeat the prayer of salvation to give your life to Jesus."

God lovingly guided and provided me with the words as she sincerely repeated her prayer. Ecstatic, Julie sensed a shift in her spirit and a connection to Jesus from that moment on. Squealing with delight, we hugged each other. Julie had more questions concerning her new faith. We spent another half an hour in her driveway as the Spirit gave me answers. Both of us were learning that unforgettable evening with God leading the way.

Now go; I will help you speak and will teach you what to say. (Exodus 4:12)

Tragedy

Months later, my daughter grabbed her backpack and headed out the front door to meet with Julie. The two were headed to another friend's house with several other girls for a sleep over.

Later that evening, two local boys drove up and invited the girls for hamburgers at a popular fast food restaurant. Julie and another friend climbed into the backseat coaxing Natalie to join them. Stooping down low to climb in, Natalie had her left foot in the car and pushed off with her right foot.

As soon as her right foot left the ground, she heard a man's harsh voice yell, "No, get out!"

Shaken and upset, she backed out of the car. While she studied everyone's face, she asked, "Who said that?"

The group was silent, shrugging and glancing around at each other. The boys urged her to climb in as they were in a hurry. She paused for a few moments, contemplating what she heard before declining their invitation. Natalie had a strong suspicion she heard the Spirit of God warn her not to get into the car. She wasn't sure. The four teens drove away.

Natalie couldn't shake her odd, troubled feeling, so she gathered her belongings and walked home. Her departure was sudden. On her long walk home in the dark she had a sinking feeling. She wondered why the Spirit warned her as she tried to analyze the situation, but came to no conclusion.

Our living room was on the small side with two beautiful white, leather sofas arranged between a refurbished whiskey barrel end table sitting in the corner with a lamp where the picture windows met. Both sofas sat arranged on two walls from the corner with red velvet throw pillows and matching throw blanket.

Waking up in her own bed late the next morning, Natalie was well rested and happy to be home. She wrapped herself in her favorite white blanket with blue accents and positioned herself comfortably on the couch looking out the windows. This was one of her favorite relaxing pastimes. As I walked through the living room, I was surprised and delighted to see her. Natalie gave me a warm hello. I sat on the other sofa to talk as I wondered why she was home.

Natalie loved home and remarked how beautiful and relaxing it was to just sit and stare out the window. By her comment, I sensed she was relieved for some reason. I felt a small and subtle check in my spirit. Something just didn't seem right and I wondered what happened the night before to make her want to walk home in the dark, so I questioned her. She gave me the lame excuse she couldn't sleep. During our talk, I sensed a troubling hesitation in her voice and mentioned this to her.

Finally, she opened up and spoke honestly. She gave me the run-down on the previous night and the warning she heard questioning if she heard the Spirit's voice to get out of the car. I agreed with her conclusion that it was the Spirit, but neither of us understood the reason for the warning.

Soon, my youngest daughter, Alicia, came out of her bedroom and sat on the floor to listen too. My niece, Sarah, walked up from my mother's house just down the street.

She and Alicia were the same age of twelve and she was spending a few weeks in Oregon with us. She joined Alicia sitting cross-legged on the carpet and listened as Natalie recalled the scene from the night before about the warning she heard from the Spirit. We talked about this at length. I told Natalie I was proud that she responded to God's request.

Natalie received a devastating phone call a few hours later at one that afternoon. Shortly after the teens left there was a terrible wreck and all four had tragically died in the single car accident. Much later, we realized the other three teenagers had lived their lives for Jesus. We discussed how Julie became a believer just a few months earlier. All four teens are in Heaven now.

———◦⊂⊱⊃◦———

It was Julie's appointed time to give her life to Jesus guaranteeing her place in Heaven just a few months later. We don't have all the answers. The big one would be why was my beautiful daughter's life was spared and not the other four teens. I wonder if they might have all been alerted to the danger as well, but didn't realize it as a word from God. Maybe Natalie was the only one who recognized the voice as that of the Spirit.

We are deeply saddened that the lives of these four teens were cut short. We won't understand until we are in Heaven as well. But we are also encouraged that God ensured they would all be in Heaven after the tragic accident.

———◦⊂⊱⊃◦———

For God so loved the world that He gave His only begotten Son, that whoever believes in Him should not perish but have everlasting life. (John 3:16)

Ask Yourself...

- *When God asks me to share Jesus with someone, am I willing and ready to do so?*
- *Do I now see it might be urgent for them as in Julie's circumstance?*
- *Do I realize if I have a willing spirit, the Spirit will give me the words?*
- *What habits can I develop, so I can spread the seeds of faith to others?*

-14-

Refusing to Compromise

Our marriage hit a very rough patch a few years after we were married. I became demanding, sarcastic and insulting while Bernie became passive-aggressive and made irrational financial decisions. We tried to muddle our way through those problems. We both created bad habits with our attitudes toward one another.

Micromanaging Bernie seemed to kill all the joy in our marriage making things worse. I couldn't come up with a good enough plan to bring us back to where we once were, happy and making good decisions together.

Bernie had seen my prophetic gift many times and the thought came to me that I could wrangle him to my way of thinking. By simply telling him, "The Lord said..." I could fill in the blanks according to my own agenda. This lie would have been a terrible betrayal to the Lord, Bernie and I.

I decided I would rather suffer in this life than taint my beautiful prophetic and seer gifts. And suffer we did!

Think about the things of Heaven, not the things of earth.
(Colossians 3:2)

Whatever we focus on we shall have it whether we speak life or death. I constantly complained that my life was difficult, my marriage was bad and we'll always be poor. I seemed to fall into the murky waters of hopelessness and despair.

I felt lost in my world of anger and self-pity. I felt helpless as I sat by and watched our world crumble. We fumbled our way through for a few years. I had enough and decided to pray and declare God's promises over our marriage.

Death and life are in the power of the tongue... (Proverbs 18:21)

Ask Yourself...

- *Have I been focusing and putting my trust in a person rather than God?*
- *What do I need to do to get back on track with God's plans for me in my relationship with Him?*
- *Do I put my focus on the promises of God rather than the problems of my life?*

-15-

Batter Up!

A few years of suffering was enough for me. My focus became crystal clear as I created a new mindset and habit to focus on God and His promises in the Bible. Realizing all the dysfunction in our marriage and finances, I went to work. Determined to focus only on the blessings I wanted in my life, I placed my problems in the background.

I rolled up my sleeves, set my mind on Jesus and became determined to enjoy my life asking God to figure out all our problems. I entered into His presence through praise and prayer while declaring scripture in our lives as a couple.

Several months later as I prayed in bed, I heard the Spirit speak two words, "Batter up!"

Being the seasoned, Christian woman who hears the Spirit speak often, I responded with a confused, "What?"

Waiting for an explanation, I held still holding my breath and listened.

I heard the same clear, distinct voice again, "Batter up!"

Not receiving further instruction I decided to take action instead. I climbed out of bed and stood in my housecoat. I shut my eyes as I obeyed the Lord who I felt was prompting me to stand in the batting stance.

With my arms up, I found my comfortable batting position moving around a bit while leaning forward with my feet in just the right position. I started to have fun and enjoyed myself, still not really understanding what was going on.

Playing baseball was a long-forgotten passion of mine. Playing on teams over the years when I was much younger, I had always been pretty good at this sport. This passion rose deep from within me again.

Seconds passed before a memory flashed in my mind. For several years, I was the star pitcher on one of the women's baseball teams I played in. I even had my picture in the newspaper once and I thought of myself as a true winner.

The Vision

Then I had a vision from God. In this precise vision, I could barely get over how great I felt, feeling and seeing *the sun* way up in the sky to my right. Bright rays of loving light consumed me, shining in all directions, but especially down toward me. I felt content and connected to the sun which I realized was a metaphor for *The Son of God, Jesus*.

The Spirit told me, "When the enemy *pitches an emotional assault* toward you, I want you to bat it way out of the park!"

God was helping me release the anger and resentment I carried in my heart for Bernie through this exercise using baseball.

The Lord and I practiced a few times first. Still shutting my eyes and enjoying this vision, I saw the *emotional assault pitched*, (being upset by Bernie), from the enemy as a baseball, so I swung hitting it easily. In my mind's eye, I watched it go to *the Son* as He dissolved it with His rays of love and light in the sky. Beautiful residue flittered in the sky like shiny dust specks floating on rays of sunshine before it completely disintegrated. What a beautiful sight, fun exercise and confidence builder! It worked perfectly and I couldn't wait to put it to good use!

My New Tool

The Spirit said, "Wasn't that easy? Wasn't that fun? That's what you can do every time you feel yourself getting upset at Bernie!"

It did seem easy and fun. Determined to use this new tool every time, I soon became mindful of my feelings. At the first sign of a bad thought toward Bernie, I almost welcomed the opportunity to nip it in the bud.

I could easily do this out in public too. I'd put my head down, my hands together and swing ever so slightly so as not to be noticed. The fun part was making the clicking sound with my tongue of the bat hitting the ball. The Lord's idea was quick, easy and made me smile at how fun this process became.

I took it to the next level and dug deep into the scriptures to find my answers. I needed to adjust my expectations and attitude about Bernie. I had become calloused due to my unfulfilled promises and broken heart.

Stop being angry! Turn from your rage!
Do not lose your temper- it only leads to harm. (Psalms 37:8)

Satan is the father of all lies and the battlefield is in our mind. He is constantly trying to convince us to believe his lies. When we establish bad habits, it's tough to set our minds on things that are good and holy. The Spirit used my love of baseball to show me I needed to train my mind to resist the enemy's attacks.

Therefore submit to God. Resist the devil and he will fee from you.
(James 4:7)

God gave me this fun exercise to use, so I could recognize my bad habit of thinking negatively about Bernie. It's a slippery slope when we justify our negative feelings about someone as we will keep looking and adding more evidence to pile on top eventually creating a mountain.

Instead of holding a mirror up in front of my face revealing who I had become, God guided me down this path as an attitude adjustment.

Ask Yourself…

- *Have I allowed myself to become judgmental and unforgiving with a loved one?*
- *When these feelings try to assault me, will I stop and ask the Lord to show me how to deal with the situation in a kind and loving way?*
- *Do I see this will mature me and bless my relationships?*

This book is a love story between the Lord and me. Are you beginning to catch a glimpse of God's love for you too? God wants you to give yourself to Him and will lovingly lead you on your own personal journey through the firestorms of life. Why not take a moment and begin to keep a journal of your own Memorable Moments? You may be surprised at what you learn as you revisit each one.

-16-

Hitchhikers

It became a memorable evening for the two of us sophisticates. I was sixteen and Lori and I were out on the town celebrating her seventeenth birthday. In our high heels, dresses and beautiful camel hair coats, we shopped a little before I bought her a fancy dinner at an expensive restaurant sitting high on a hill overlooking down-town Portland. We enjoyed watching the beautiful lights flickering on the river.

Driving my dad's new Mercedes Benz, we were both trying to appear and act older as the cultured and refined teens we were that evening. We hoped onlookers saw two successful businesswomen instead of two teens in Daddy's fancy car.

We enjoyed a wonderful evening and on the way home we laughed and reminisced swapping old childhood stories as we'd known each other since grade school.

It was nearly ten o'clock on that Friday night and Lori and I were chatting away on the highway heading toward home. I heard the Spirit direct me to pick up the hitchhikers on the road that we'd see in a few minutes. I didn't see them yet, but knew it was going to be soon. I told Lori what I heard. Lori hadn't experienced my prophetic gift and didn't understand what was happening. She became terribly upset shaking her head in disagreement. She didn't have a say in this decision and I informed her as much.

Our first thoughts were neither of us wanted a couple of dirty, sweaty guys in our car. She reluctantly agreed to pick up whoever we came across on the freeway.

After that conversation, I heard the Spirit tell me, "The two hitchhikers are in grave danger as there is another vehicle a few minutes behind you. If you don't stop and pick them up, they won't live through the night."

I didn't understand my assignment and had no idea who they were, but confident I would stop for them. God indicated that I was to save their lives that night. My mind wandered as I created terrible images of what we might see on the road. What came to mind was two dirty thugs who were beaten and bloody who were trying to escape other dirty thugs and all of them were up to no good.

Within two minutes, we were shocked and understood the word from the Spirit. The hitchhikers weren't scruffy men like I envisioned. They were two giggling, pretty, blonde fourteen-year-old girls hitchhiking late at night. I pulled over and without a thought for their safety they hopped right in.

These pampered little girls were wearing extreme miniskirts, high heels, tight blouses and too much makeup. They dressed a bit rough, but by their actions I concluded they were naïve and reckless little girls headed for big trouble. Their innocence made me see them as many years younger than I, even though we were only two years apart in age. It was evident they were extremely unwise and I could see why God had me come to their aid.

I asked them where they wanted to be dropped off and they gave me directions. Lori and I rolled our eyes at each other at how silly and foolish these little girls were acting with total disregard to their safety. We listened to them brag about their adventures of hitchhiking all over Portland, going to parties and hopping into anyone's car who stopped along the freeways. I was horrified by their ongoing, foolish actions knowing they were flirting with disaster.

This was their activity every Friday night as the parents went to bed early in exhaustion from working all week. They were sharing all kinds of intimate details about their escapades. Lori and I were pretending we thought it was funny with fake grins plastered on our faces. After we dropped them off, I saw the window they crawled back into.

Idling on the side of the street, I sat angry at their dangerous little game while pondering my next move. I felt a check in my spirit that I needed to take this a step further as I fumed with anger. Realizing the Lord saved their lives that night I took it upon myself to alert the parents of that important fact.

I parked the car in the driveway with the headlights pointing directly into the living room window and honked the horn for a few minutes. I saw another light come on in this gorgeous, white home with pillars inside and out.

Leaving Lori loudly protesting in the car, I boldly walked up to the front door. I stood pressing my finger against the doorbell listening to it ring over and over as I glanced at this ritzy neighborhood with expensive homes.

A few minutes later, both parents came to the door in their housecoats wondering what all the commotion was outside. They opened the door and I immediately barged right in to take care of business, stopping all this dangerous nonsense.

Standing inside the elegant foyer of this grand home, I was nauseously angry and upset about both girls. I introduced myself as the person who just picked up their two hitchhiking girls on the highway, dropped off them off at this house and watched them climb in the bedroom window.

From their behavior, the parents were clearly upset. The father politely asked me to stop speaking for a moment as he rushed down the hall to his daughter's room.

The furious, red faced father came back with his frightened daughter and her friend, still dressed in their shameless attire. All four of them listened as I reported all the details of that night. Both of the girls stood there with such hateful looks of betrayal on their faces as I relayed all the stories including the intimate details these girls gave me. What a killjoy I was that night!

━━━━━━━━━◦⊂⋙⊃◦━━━━━━━━━

I explained in detail to all four of them how God spoke to me urging me to pick the hitchhikers up even before I saw the girls on the highway. The parents heard how God told me the girls' lives were in danger and I was to rescue them from a night ending in grave disaster.

As you can imagine, the parents were very grateful and assured me change was on the horizon. I felt great knowing they were safe again under God's and the parents' protection again. They all saw a side of God they might not have seen before and had a lot to think about that night.

━━━━━━━━━◦⊂⋙⊃◦━━━━━━━━━

"For I know the plans I have for you," says the Lord.
"They are plans for good and not for disaster,
to give you a future and a hope." (Jeremiah 29:11)

Ask Yourself...

- *Has God ever used me to step in and change a potentially dangerous situation?*
- *Do I have the boldness and confidence to do something out of the norm if I hear God's voice instructing me to do so?*
- *Have I ever felt holy anger from God regarding a dangerous situation becoming involved until it was resolved?*
- *What were the circumstances and how were things changed?*
- *What would I do next time?*

Valerie

Bernie and I were exhausted from working hard all day. All we wanted to do was eat, shower and throw our exhausted bodies in bed. We landed in bed at eight that night and collapsed. I lay there silently staring into the dark while enjoying the rest, but waiting for sleep. Bernie was asleep as soon as his head hit the pillow. I watched the headlights of passing cars flickering on the ceiling through the leaves of the swaying trees as they passed by. It created the usual peaceful atmosphere I loved. I dozed off within minutes.

A short time later, I was awakened by the Spirit, wide awake. God had a beautiful message for my friend, Valerie. He asked me to tell her to have faith and hope and all her problems would work out as He has a glorious plan for her life.

God's message was sweet and loving and it moved my heart in a big way. I was still in my bed with my eyes shut savoring all the loving affirmations God was giving me for her. He said I was to email Valerie the next morning and express these sentiments.

Then the Lord instructed me, "Look at the clock and when you email her, tell her what time it is now."

I knew this was some kind of secret that Valerie and God shared and was the most important part of the letter.

I glanced at the clock and the orange numbers glowed "10:10." Aha, I thought, it's clear to me! All I had to do was to figure out what book of the Bible this scripture was from and I'd have the message too. With my eyes shut, I thought about it for a few minutes, but nothing came to mind as I drifted off to sleep again.

At that same time, Valerie laid in bed agonizing over her problems. She was conflicted and not sure of the direction to take. Her troubled marriage stifled her physically and emotionally as she felt depressed and downtrodden. Things were getting progressively worse and her heart was heavy and dull. Her inability to sleep and poor eating habits were wearing on her emotions. She found even the simple things in life difficult to accomplish.

Valerie had enough of her pity party and turned to God in prayer. Her prayers lasted most of the night which was evident by the dark circles under her eyes the next day.

Early that morning, I emailed her giving her all the loving sentiments from God. The last thing I wrote in the email was about 10:10. I told her I couldn't figure out this Bible verse and asked her to tell me, so I could be blessed too.

She immediately called me telling me she was so touched by God's email and saw it as a response to her prayers. God woke me at the same time Valerie became upset caving in to fear and worry. She confessed she had been awake most of the night worrying about problems she had no control over.

Valerie had been praying late into the morning. Her response took my breath away and I was blessed to deliver this message to my friend. When she read about the secret code of 10:10 she laughed and cried with joy. Valerie's love letter came with God's secret message for her as a confirmation of her value to Him as 10:10 is actually her birthday!

This is a great example of stepping out of our comfort zone when we think we might have a word for someone. God sometimes speaks to us loudly and sometimes He speaks to us in a whisper. I'm glad I took a few minutes to deliver this word to Valerie as she felt cared for and blessed.

*The Lord is close to the brokenhearted; he rescues
those whose spirits are crushed...*
(Psalms 34:18)

Ask Yourself...

- *Do I have the faith in God that He is working behind the scenes on my behalf?*
- *Do I pray and expect God will take care of me too?*
- *Am I willing to pray and ask God to give me words for others?*
- *If so, am I willing to deliver them even when I don't understand the meaning?*

-18-

Mom's Nightmare

Mom woke up with a jolt as she laid in bed feeling nauseous. A minute later, she turned over to check the time. It was well after four in the morning, a little too late to fall back to sleep again. She was still groggy, emotionally drained from the anguish and panic of her recurring nightmare. Her chin trembled with fear. Her freshly washed sheets were drenched in sweat again. *Ugh, like I need more work today,* she thought knowing she already had a full day taking care of the house and us three kids.

She gingerly crawled out of bed allowing Dad to continue sleeping. Her legs were jittery from the emotional turmoil of her recurring nightmare and her walk was unsteady. She felt clumsy as she fumbled her way to the hook on the back of the bedroom door where her housecoat hung. Trying to shake off the effects of her nightmare, her plan each time was to power through the fear and start her normal routine for the day.

Throwing her light blue, terry cloth housecoat over her dampened night gown, she slipped on her new slippers and plodded down the stairs. She scuffed down the hardwood floors of the long hall toward the kitchen with every other step a slight squeak of the old, scuffed boards.

Starting a pot of coffee, she took out the toaster and headed toward the counter where her homemade bread was freshly cut the day before. *Maybe something to eat will settle my stomach,* she thought as she slipped a piece of bread into the toaster and pushed the lever down. Her anxiety eased with each moment she fiddled in the kitchen. She glanced at the clock and ran her fingers through her curly, black hair several times to soothe her nerves.

The same recurring nightmare haunted her three times a year for the last several years. It tormented her with the exact details and frightening results each time and seemed more like a real event than a dream. Mom couldn't understand why.

It was in the late 1950's and Mom was in her thirties. Mom was part Blackfeet Indian and was always very thin and pretty with a sweet disposition. We lived in upstate New York in a huge, historic house.

The Nightmare

Mom and the three of us kids were driving to the beach for a day in a newer, white Plymouth. Mom could feel the excitement as we were off to explore our new, unfamiliar surroundings. The landscape and trees were quite different from those in our home region of upstate New York.

In this nightmare, she had the sense that we had moved far from our home and we were exploring our new state. Mom noticed a sign for a picnic area and a trail for hiking. Without notice, she veered off the highway. As we drove, we heard the muffled, crunching sound of the gravel under our tires against the dirt road. All four of us smiled with excitement knowing we were off on another adventure with Mom leading the way.

She admired the scenery of the tall hills covered in lush, green trees. We parked the car and marveled at the beauty of the landscape with a few streams which trickled crystal clear water in the small green meadow. Purple, orange and yellow wild flowers sprung up in the grass which created a picturesque scene. Mom stood there with her hands on her hips as she breathed in all the fresh mountainous air awestruck by the beauty. Mom was aware she was using all of her senses as she scanned the layout of the area.

Off to the far side were two outhouses and some garbage cans. On the other side were picnic tables and in the middle was the trail head zigzagging its way toward the top of the irresistibly beautiful mountain.

She could see other families strolling happily along the trail enjoying the cool air of spring. Mom stood observing the trail. She noticed the tree line of a distant mountain shaped like a woman's profile face up. A few distinguishing, craggy rocks of the cliffs were where an earring might be. Mom smiled, relaxed and content.

She brought the basket from the trunk of the car. Shaking the white tablecloth printed with bright red lobsters she spread it out on the old, wooden picnic table before arranging our individual place settings as if preparing for fine dining. Mom always made a meticulous lunch and eating in this beautiful setting created a tranquil and charming atmosphere which we were enjoying.

After lunch, the four of us started the trek up the trail and the further we hiked the steeper and narrower the trail became. Mom became concerned as she watched my older brother, Frank, hiking way too fast and too far ahead. This was typical for most thirteen-year-old boys who love to explore.

Mom could see the trail had become more dangerous and she cupped her hands around her mouth to call out. He was too far ahead and couldn't hear. She told my sister and me to stop where we stood as she raced up the trail to catch Frank. She wanted to end the hike and turn back due to the unsafe terrain.

Finally, Mom became close enough to Frank, who finally heard her yelling for him to stop. As Frank turned to glance her way, his feet slipped on some small pebbles. She watched him as he fell, disappearing from her view far below.

At this point, she always woke up feeling nauseated, sweaty and frightened.

The Hike – Years Later

Years later we moved from upstate New York to Oregon in the early 1960s. One spring day we were on our way to the beach. As in the dream, Mom took the exit off the highway to investigate a picnic area and a hiking trail.

Mom packed a huge lunch with crab salad sandwiches, fresh fruit, cookies and water. As in the nightmare, she spread out our picnic tablecloth patterned with drawings of lobsters. Mom bought this tablecloth in her home state of Maine years earlier and just the mere sight of it always brought fond memories to my mind. We enjoyed every morsel of the lunch she packed. The best tasting food was always eaten outside as hiking and fresh air always made us hungry. After we cleaned the table, we were excited to hike the trail up the side of the mountain.

Not too far into our hike, Mom had a bad feeling about our situation. Mentioning she sensed danger lurking about, she couldn't put her finger on what might be wrong. She asked us to stop hiking. Mom tried to dismiss her doubts when a feeling of déjà vu washed over her. We observed Mom as she became hyper-vigilant. Clenching her jaw she narrowed her eyes shading them with her hand from the bright morning sun. She slowly surveyed the area hoping to make sense of this uneasy feeling.

I stood somber to stare at Mom as I observed her quick, jerky steps as she slowly backed away from the edge of the trail trying to spot any danger. All four of us were standing on the narrowing dirt path just a five-minute hike up from the trailhead as it looped and winded up the mountain. We stood and watched as her eyes paused at the tree line on the next mountain over. She saw the woman's face with rocky boulders for earrings. She recognized this mountainous feature as part of the scene from her recurring nightmare.

Mom suddenly shuddered as she became aware these nightmares had always been warnings to her. Not having a relationship with God she couldn't figure out where the series of warnings came from. In a shaky voice, she yelled at us three kids to carefully head back down the trail toward the car. Clearing her throat, she explained this was the scene of her recurring nightmare, the one we listened to many times over the past six years.

Walking swiftly down the trail that day, a spiritual shift happened within me as I realized I walked in the light of God's truth. Mom walked in spiritual darkness. I saw the truth that the Lord was the author of these nightmares as warnings to save my brother. The Lord had to make His warnings extremely obvious and often enough for her to recognize this event when it unfolded before her eyes in real life.

Catching sight of her frightened and eerie expression, I noticed she bore the same wild look she gave me each time I spoke of my Holy Spirit encounters. I finally understood Mom had never rejected me, but had no awareness of God's presence in her life or mine. I always had a clear understanding that my hearing God's voice, seeing visions or how I just knew things was God interacting with me. I always happily obeyed God, but Mom was clueless and I felt sad for her.

Our struggle is not against flesh and blood, but against the spiritual forces of evil in the heavenly realms. (Ephesians 6:12)

The enemy's fear came roaring in on the heels of Mom's understanding that her dreams had always been warnings to her. Mom believed the lies of the enemy that these dreams were from the devil and not from God which doesn't make sense because Frank was saved.

The devil is the author of fear and confusion and overwhelmed her by delivering a powerful punch of terror and confusion straight into her heart. I witnessed this in the physical back then by her nearly panicked expression and sharp movements.

Not having a relationship with the Lord, Mom was spiritually and emotionally defenseless against the enemy's attacks. God was waiting for her to call to him. Even a whispered, "Jesus, help me," would have changed her situation. God would have stepped in, fear and confusion would flee and she would have given God all the glory for saving Frank.

Unfortunately, the mere mention of this incident was frightening to her until she gave her life to Jesus fifty years later when she finally understood the things of God.

For God has not given us a spirit of fear, but of power, love and a sound mind. (2 Timothy 1:7)

Now I understand this a little more in the spiritual realm too. I was grateful and relieved God saved my brother knowing this incident was in the past. She was frightened and confused for most of the day and all I could do was watch her with pity and keep my mouth shut. Even at ten years of age I understood my faith was from God. Mom's fear was from the enemy.

Mom spoke of the series of nightmares and our hike for the rest of her life. When I suggested it was God who gave her these dreams as a warning she would immediately dismiss my explanation and change the subject.

The enemy stole God's glory for saving Frank's life. Mom believed the enemy's lies that he was the one giving her the dreams of warning. He won that small victory for keeping Mom in fear.

Ask Yourself...

- *Have I been warned of impending danger, not realizing until later it was God?*
- *Am I training myself to listen and be aware of the Spirit's voice?*
- *Am I ready to shift my thinking, so I can recognize that the Spirit does talk to me and wants to use my talents?*
- *Am I ready to create a new habit of thanking God out loud when I see His hand in my life to shift my thinking?*
- *What might happen in my walk with God if I do this on a regular basis?*

Section Three:

Medical Challenges

So you shall serve the Lord your God, and He will bless your bread
and your water. And I will take sickness away from
the midst of you. (Exodus 23:25)

-19-

Firefighter

Stepping Out of My Comfort Zone

Constantly praying to God that I would be healed of fibromyalgia, I put one foot in front of the other most days. With brain fog, migraines and terrible pain all over my body, I tried to ignore the harsh reality that having a normal life again may be impossible. I've heard fibromyalgia is caused by deep feelings of hopelessness and despair brought on by a perceived lack of nurturing and protection from childhood trauma.

Suffering the most were my three children who had a mother constantly begging, "Please be quiet and let me rest here on the couch."

Adriene was probably one of my only good friends at the time. She had me pumped up and excited to attend a class for a CERT (Community Emergency Response Team) at our little town's local fire station.

My children were adults by this time, but it was still difficult for me to go anywhere or do much of anything. I was determined to go to the CERT classes, so I'd prepare by taking migraine medicine before each class. Adriene's schedule changed at the last minute and she bailed on me, so I was on my own and determined to attend. I was stepping out in faith to challenge myself to see if I could handle this tough class.

After many months of training, our big mock disaster test day had arrived. The group was excited and nervous at the same time as we had worked very hard to gain the skills required to help our victims if we were ever needed.

The class of thirty voted me Chief and I was in charge. What an honor! My first order of business was to appoint another guy I felt was more qualified for the position and enjoy being part of the team. The firefighters marked down every good and bad thing we did.

At the beginning of the disaster, I turned off the blaring radio as I didn't want the loud sound to give me a migraine. I turned off a motor for the same reason and put out a small fire using the fire extinguisher. Within three minutes, I had three points! I scored the highest marks in the class. As a group we all did poorly as expected, but we learned so much through our mistakes.

Following the Holy Spirit's Instructions

In the training room after the mock disaster, one of the officers had two volunteer firefighter applications. He said he saw great qualities and natural abilities in two people and he claimed he was never wrong when evaluating who might become a great volunteer. He slapped one of the applications in front of me and the second application went to the one I appointed as our chief. He told the two of us not to leave without filling them out.

I sat at the desk staring at the application. What an honor to have been chosen! But due to my poor health, I couldn't see it happening for me.

I heard the Spirit clearly speak, "Fill out the application and believe you aren't sick."

Quickly scribbling the information on the application, I handed it in and left for home. Months went by and I finally received a letter in the mail telling me the process to pick volunteers would start soon.

The Lord told me, "Go through the process and see what happens."

The first step was to have a face-to-face interview with four other firefighters. I had six weeks to slim down and get in better shape before the interview. I was actually playing the part knowing they wouldn't pick me anyway. I was forty-seven-years-old with fibromyalgia, but I exercised and buffed up for the interview.

The Spirit told me, "Ignore your disability and speak as though you are totally healed."

Okay, I thought to myself, *I can have fun with this interview. I feel like a fraud, but the Lord is telling me to disregard my disability and jump right in.*

... and call those things that do not exist as though they did.
(Romans 4:17)

I started declaring, "I declare that I am a great volunteer firefighter!"

Knowing my only task was to listen, believe and obey the Lord, I spoke these words out loud to cover the fibromyalgia symptoms. I was following God who was urging me to keep going and that I wasn't wasting anyone's time.

In the waiting room before the interview, I saw four other men who were tall, built like lumberjacks, tough and twenty years my junior. I relaxed and waited my turn thinking I didn't have a chance against these men, so why worry.

During the interview, they asked me what I was afraid of and a series of questions pertaining to my capabilities.

I was relaxed and gave my smug answer, "To die without true love."

They all laughed and asked me if I was afraid of fire, heights, blood, or seeing injured people on the road. I answered no to each and had to comment on why I knew I wasn't afraid of these things.

"Fire is to be respected, but I've always been brave. Heights? I jump off fifty foot bridges and cliffs into the water and call it fun. Injured people? I have seen a young man cut his fingers off and was the only one able to help him. Also, I'm a mom, so I've seen my share of injuries, blood and whatnot."

Healing Me Physically and Emotionally

Laughing, they thanked me for the interview as though I had done well. I had a new attitude about myself and a glimmer of hope for my future as these professionals seemed to appreciate me and saw value in my abilities. I saw myself more worthy of a real life as the Lord kept encouraging me through this process.

Months later, I received the letter which stated I had been chosen as one of four out of the twenty eight applicants.

The Lord kept urging me, "Keep going!"

I buffed up and trimmed down even more as we were expected to report to a neighboring fire house and start our rigorous training in a few weeks.

We were to train sometimes in ninety-eight degree weather outside while we wore our full gear. My partner was a buff, young man about twenty years younger. All that grueling and intense training was so much fun. Following God's guidance gave me all the confidence I needed to do my best and be successful in my new endeavor.

Combating Fear, God's Way

One training exercise was particularly grueling. I laughingly deemed this *the claustrophobic weed out*. The training officers instructed us to put on our turnouts (firefighting clothing) and SCBAs, (self contained breathing apparatus). Without informing us first, they duct taped our masks on to prevent us from seeing or pulling them off. They also duct taped our gloves to the sleeves of our jackets. We stood there as they blinded us and took away our sense of touch as we waited, strapped into a breathing apparatus. Sensory deprivation of not being able to breathe fresh air and not being able to see or feel anything is a great scare tactic especially when we were carrying an extra sixty pounds of gear on our backs and dressed in our turnouts.

Soon my mind became accustomed to this sensory deprivation as I kept whispering to myself, "Thank you, Jesus!" I became determined and fearless again.

The officers laughed as they turned motors on, blasted us with big gusts of air and blared loud horns right over our heads. This exercise was to simulate the worst case scenario we would inevitably run into on the job and we needed to be prepared.

We were given our instructions to crawl following each other. I was the lead person in charge of the others behind me. Each person behind me was holding a piece of equipment while holding onto the pant leg of the person crawling in front of them, so we wouldn't get separated one from another.

At some point, it was my responsibility to crawl around by myself and find the unfortunate unconscious victim in this simulation. The building was huge and all my senses were dulled other than my sense of hearing.

The only other woman out of thirty six trainees was directly behind me. This felt like a setup for us women, but I was determined to do well. After a minute or so she started screaming hysterically and trying to tear her gear off. My determination level was maxed out when I heard her frantically pleading with the officers to pull the tape off of her. The officers made her calm down before doing so as she was uncontrollably claustrophobic. She was excused from the program and left angry pointing her finger at me.

They told me, "Keep moving, keep moving, go get that unconscious man or he'll die!"

While crawling on the floor with my axe, I found this large man and pulled him out by the back collar of his shirt to safety. Not good. His collar became dangerously tight around the front of his neck, he was choking and making terrible faces. Everyone silently laughed and I took a little heat from that mistake.

The training was physically demanding and strenuous. The day of the final test day was upon us. Being in my late forties, I was the oldest person at the firefighter academy and had recently become the only woman. The final test comprised of pulling ladders off the truck and running them to the wall of the building where we would correctly tie them for safety. We were to hoist a chainsaw to the top of the building, start it and stop it, then finally display knot tying abilities to lower it back down, all the while my partner was doing similar things. I didn't know we were being timed, so I slowed down at the end. As I strolled across the finish line everyone was yelling for me to hurry.

If I hadn't slowed down, we would have been first, but Josh and I took second place in the class. I became an official volunteer firefighter making seven dollars a call and I was so delighted!

God used this training to heal me emotionally and physically and I had no symptoms of fibromyalgia over the next four years.

Skills for Everyday Life

God has used my skills occasionally at the scene of a few car and bike accidents. I have taken control of accident scenes where people were severely injured.

Several times I have heard bystanders say, "Let's pull them out of the car and stand them up!"

The group of untrained, but good hearted people would start heading for the injured. I have jumped in to stop this kind of action, declared I was an ex-firefighter and asked everyone to stand back until the fire department arrived.

I heard the Spirit prompt me, "Keep going! Don't worry, I have it all under control!" Training at the firefighting academy was something I enjoyed as I'd always seen myself being physically adept and agile. I was a tough lady and stopped worrying and started to become all that again.

Trust in the Lord with all your heart; do not depend on your own understanding. Seek his will in all you do, and he will show you which path to take. (Proverbs 3:5-6)

Ask Yourself...

- *Has God ever asked me to try something I thought I could not do?*
- *What did I find out about myself and God when I stepped out in faith?*
- *How did it turn out?*
- *How can I turn this into my personal testimony to help others see God's hand in their own lives?*

-20-

Firefighting Ambassadors

As a rookie firefighter, my first emergency call to one of our town's fine senior assisted living residences in the middle of the night and was memorable for me. Those older folks were more interested in having company to visit with than they were in the reason for the emergency.

We rushed down the halls. The residents moved and aligned their wheelchairs or stood right in the middle of the hall. They were hoping we would have to squeeze by, so they could touch us as we jogged past them. The residents were trying to slow us down for a reason I didn't understand yet.

Ambassadors of Love

I noticed these faithful firefighters giving each other meaningful glances as we walked through the maze of people and wheelchairs. After the emergency, we were walking toward the exit. I observed my fellow firefighters taking off their gloves, shoving them in their pockets and holding their helmets under their arms.

These tough firefighters yielded themselves to the love of Jesus which overflowed into the whole atmosphere. Despite being two in the morning, those Christian men knelt down and lovingly offered the residents a few moments of friendly chit-chat. They held the old folks' hands and gazed deeply in their eyes to talk and listen.

This was the defining moment. This interaction was what God wanted me to witness. This was how the godly senior firefighters extended Jesus' love each time we walked those halls. Those special times will be forever highlighted in my heart – the whole atmosphere was filled with the Spirit of God and those residents were hungry and waiting for another godly encounter through my fellow firefighters. What a lesson!

Imitate me, just as I also imitate Christ. (1 Corinthians 11:1)

Those heroes in the night offered sweet words of tenderness from their hearts to soothe the lonely hearts of the residents. I witnessed their eyes sparkle as they were talkative and enthusiastic for this interaction because of these great men of God. Those officers became my heroes as I jumped right in and did the same thing until it was time to go.

For God is not unjust; He will not forget your work and the labor of love which you have shown toward His name, in that you have ministered to the saints, and do minister. (Hebrews 6:10)

Another paramedic/firefighter received phone calls every Saturday night from an elderly woman wanting to bring her ailing husband into the fire station. She was only slightly better off than her husband. This young firefighter always made himself available to this couple to give them a quick going over. I'd often see this young man in his early thirties come to the station on his off hours to care for them.

The real draw was the love and attention he offered them so generously. The rest of the staff always came by to warmly greet them like old friends. The elderly man and woman seemed to relax and laugh with eyes that just sparkled.

And do everything with love. (1 Corinthians 16:14)

Going to the hospital always included hours of waiting in an uncomfortable atmosphere, so this was much more pleasant. At the fire station, they would get a warm welcome and a cup of hot cocoa. It was easy to see this elderly man and his loving wife didn't have too much money.

———————— ◦◦⟨⟨⟨⟩◦◦ ————————

This young paramedic would get down on one knee and deal with not only the older man, but check the wife too. She mildly protested with a shy smile and a twinkle in her eye, so grateful for the love and attention.

His actions gave this older couple the confidence they were in good enough health to carry on for another week. This was against the rules, but no laws were ever broken and our fire station served God over man every time.

Those godly men demonstrated Jesus' love to everyone they encountered and never left home without their faith. This was their mission and I know they prayed early in the mornings to that end. I believe this was the reason God wanted me to become a volunteer firefighter… so I could learn what imitating Jesus really looked like. I salute them and all they taught me!

———————— ◦◦⟨⟨⟨⟩◦◦ ————————

And the King will say, I tell you the truth, when you did it to one of the least of these my brothers and sisters, you were doing it to me!
(Matthew 25:40)

Ask Yourself…

- *Do I remember to bring my faith with me at all times?*
- *What small acts of kindness can I do to make a difference in someone's day?*
- *Can I be more kind and loving to all?*
- *Do I remember a time when someone gave me extra attention when I needed special attention?*
- *What were the circumstances and results?*

-21-

Cancer Answer

Afeeling of contentment washed over me as a breeze blew in
from the kitchen window. I was enjoying washing the breakfast dishes. It was a warm morning in early May and I glanced over
at Bernie who was reading the Sunday newspaper in the living room.
Glancing out the window, I took a moment to consider my feelings.

Bernie and I had been married for seven years, we were living in
Portland and I was fifty-five-years-old. Things weren't going so well
for us financially and I had a lot of anxiety about our future. I was
grateful and happy, trying to hide my feelings of uncertainty about
our life together. With a grateful heart there seemed to be such peace
in our house that I hadn't experienced for quite a while. I suspected it
was because I was reading my Bible more and spending time with God.

Despite all our obstacles, I truly wanted to believe what I was
praying as I whispered, "Thank you, Lord, life is going okay for us
and we're going to make it in spite of all our setbacks. I want to have
hope again for a great life and a future with Bernie, Lord. It's been hard.
Forgive me for not always being my best through these difficult times."

I Heard the Spirit Speak

In that instant, I heard the Spirit tell me in an audible voice, "Buy
the water machine."

My friend had been selling these high pH water machines for a few months and having great success helping people with big health problems.

I told Bernie what I had heard as he instantly stood and folded his newspaper declaring, "Well, we should get one today!"

A few days after we installed our water machine, Bernie asked me to see a doctor. For several months, I had been noticing a lump on my abdomen that protruded below my left rib cage in the front. It didn't hurt, but I knew it was there. Bernie had been noticing for a month that I didn't seem healthy as I started losing a lot of weight and my skin was gray and hanging loose.

Kidney Cancer Found

I made an appointment with my primary care physician. After a series of appointments and CAT scans over two days, a surgeon showed me in great detail that I had late stage four kidney cancer.

The doctor said that my left kidney had died about nine months earlier. I had a six-pound, blood filled, cancerous tumor that he felt was ready to burst. If it did burst I would bleed internally and die a horrible, painful death. The doctor told me I needed to have it removed right away. I had a triple death sentence as my living kidney, liver and lungs were at late stage four cancer as well.

The doctor was careful to point to all the cancerous, dark spots on most of my organs as we studied the CAT scan on the computer screen. I remained calm and took notes.

After half an hour, I stopped him from speaking and asked him seriously, "So the bottom line is death, death and more death, right?"

He sadly nodded in agreement.

He wanted to schedule the much needed operation which would buy me another six months or so, but told me not to expect to live to see Christmas.

The doctor said I would be in the hospital for about three weeks. He said I was going to have an extreme amount of pain for those three weeks and that I should expect it to be terrible. After the operation, they would put me in a critical care unit to watch me for a week as drain tubes would be inserted and I'd have to lay still. I would be in a regular hospital bed for another few weeks.

I nodded with understanding of what he said, but I certainly didn't agree with his prognosis. God had already shown up several weeks before the problem reared its ugly head with the cancer answer. I didn't know what was going to happen, but knew God was still on the throne. After all, I had unfulfilled promises, so I believed I would not only survive, but I was one hundred percent sure I would thrive and all the prophecies about me would be fulfilled.

The doctor concluded the consultation by saying he already consulted an oncologist who said chemo and radiation weren't an option. The cancer was already too far advanced and had spread to most of my other organs.

Doctor Doubts God

This was on Friday at five o'clock and he wanted to schedule the operation for the next Monday early in the morning.

The Lord had other plans as I heard the Spirit casually say, "No, don't be in a rush about the operation. I'll let you know when."

I calmly told the doctor, "No, Monday won't work for me. I'll let you know as I need some time to think about this."

What I was actually thinking is that I needed more time to pray to take care of this properly. The doctor told me he could see I was in shock as I was too calm and didn't understand much of what he told me. I told him I understood everything he explained.

He asked, "What did I say then?"

My response was, "You want to do a radical, left nephrectomy, remove the six-pound tumor on Monday, I have a triple death sentence in my other kidney, liver and lungs as the cancer had metastasized to most of my other organs and I won't live to see Christmas."

With total frustration, the doctor asked, "Why are you so calm after I gave you such devastating news? And how do you know those medical terms?"

I was trained in medical terminology years earlier and being a firefighter was another plus.

Not mentioning my background, I pointed up to Heaven and calmly said, "God's in control and I need to pray more about this situation."

The frustrated doctor stood up and using colorful language indicated he wasn't believer and if I was smart I would only listen to him. He certainly did insult my faith, but worse, he insulted the Lord.

I detected a strong note of disapproval in his voice as he stood over me trying to set me straight. He offered me his best advice that he was the only one able to help me. God and my prayers wouldn't help.

Without looking up at him, I calmly raised my hand in a gesture for him to stop as I said, "Moving on, doctor, moving on!"

Calmly gathering my notebook and purse, I walked out without a word. I didn't think I was well liked by him after that conversation.

Do you see that faith was working together with his works, and by words faith was made perfect? (James 2:22)

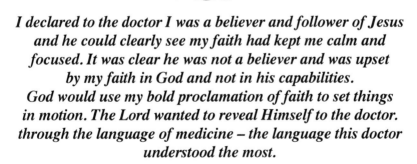

I declared to the doctor I was a believer and follower of Jesus and he could clearly see my faith had kept me calm and focused. It was clear he was not a believer and was upset by my faith in God and not in his capabilities. God would use my bold proclamation of faith to set things in motion. The Lord wanted to reveal Himself to the doctor. through the language of medicine – the language this doctor understood the most.

> *And the peace of God, which surpasses all understanding, will guard your hearts and minds in Christ Jesus.* (Philippians 4:7)

I had so much peace at this time. Smiling in my car on the way home from the doctor's office, I was thinking that most people would have been crying and begging the doctor to help them, begging for chemo or radiation. I sat there calm and collected. No wonder he was upset with me. I didn't play my part correctly as he could clearly see I had my faith in God and not his expertise.

Telling the Family

I told Bernie as soon as I arrived home and thought he had the same faith I had. He didn't. I called my daughter, Alicia, who seemed to take the news fairly well. It appeared they could see the facts as I saw them. However, I found out later that this bad news depressed her.

Hours later, I spoke with my other daughter, Natalie, and told her the news. Natalie rushed over later by herself. She came in through the back door and into my kitchen. She stopped dead in her tracks as our eyes met. Natalie stood there and stared at me without a word from the kitchen while I sat calmly on the loveseat. With such horror written across her face, I've never seen such sad eyes and to this day it still haunts me.

She finally asked me point blank, "Did God say you wouldn't die?"

I wanted to lie to spare her from such worry, but I couldn't lie. I truthfully answered her saying God didn't tell me that in so many words, but I knew I would be fine because He told me three weeks earlier to buy the water machine which would take care of the cancer.

I tried to reason with her about the facts as I saw them. I still had several unfulfilled personal prophecies, so I couldn't die! Nobody was buying into my faith, but I couldn't wait to show them how fast I would be healed.

> *For we walk by faith, not by sight.* (2 Corinthians 5:7)

The Lord created me to be competitive and I like a good challenge. He seemed to be using my competitive edge to help me fight.

I decided I wanted another great testimony revealing God's greatness to my family hoping they would all give their lives to Jesus.

I called my son, Duane, in Taiwan and my brother, Frank, to tell them the bad news. They both said they'd fly out to be with me. Three days after the diagnosis, we were expecting Frank, Duane, Uncle Bob and Aunt Inez to show up. Bernie and I had the weekend to ourselves.

I called my bedridden mother and she was devastated too, stating she would be praying for me. I never heard Mom speak of praying and I was delighted by her offer and told her as much.

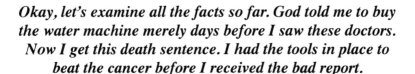

Okay, let's examine all the facts so far. God told me to buy the water machine merely days before I saw these doctors. Now I get this death sentence. I had the tools in place to beat the cancer before I received the bad report.

Within a week's time I found out I was at late stage four kidney cancer, we were possibly losing our home again, so I filed for bankruptcy to stop that action and I had started a short sale on our home. Things can't get any worse, so how can I be so calm and joyful? Faith in the face of all those struggles!

In light of all this, I prayed and sang songs of praise all the way home from the doctor's appointment. I wasn't worried at all and found it strange how much I trusted the Lord through all of this bad news.

Ask Yourself...

- *How have trials and tribulations helped build my own faith in God?*
- *How have they helped build the faith in those around me?*
- *How can I help others see God's love through me?*

-22-

Touched By An Angel

Bernie and I went to church that Sunday. Service was about to begin as Bernie and I walked in and greeted a few friends as though all was well. There was no going back, my life had changed forever. We glanced at each other then turned our attention to the pastor. We decided not to tell our friends at church until later giving us some time to make a plan. I changed my mind and wanted prayer. I was waiting for the pastor to turn the microphone on and planned to stand up and ask all of our church members to pray for me.

The Spirit responded calmly, "Settle down and don't say anything. I'll let you know when to speak."

I had confidence I would be fine, so I forgot about the doctor's report and enjoyed the service.

Bernie left the service early to play poker with his family which he did most Sundays. We were to meet them later, so I could tell them too.

At the end of church the pastor grinned and told everyone to have a great week.

I thought, *What about me, Lord?* The pastor turned off the microphone and everyone started to leave.

Nova Delivers a Word for Me

Our keyboard musician, Nova, ran to the microphone. She was bent over and zigzagging like she was avoiding sniper fire. With a strained expression, she behaved as though she saw the enemy crest the hill ready to attack.

Nova often had words for the church or individuals as she was rock solid in her faith.

She grabbed the microphone from the stand, turned it on and in a loud voice yelled, "Everybody, stop! The Lord told me someone in here got a terrible report from the doctor about their kidney! Stand up as God wants you to heal!"

After Nova prayed over me, I explained the situation to the whole church. Shocked, I could see by their expressions they were sad as they believed I was going to die. I was touched by everyone's concern, hugs and well wishes. I was disappointed by their disbelief about me not living through cancer.

Be doers of the word, and not hearers only, deceiving yourselves.
(James 1:22)

I cried as I felt such love and concern by my friends at our little church. While everyone was cleaning and putting chairs away, I made my way to the back of the room. I rested my head with my hands covering my face in an attempt to compose myself and stop crying.

Despite recent setbacks, I was waiting for my miracles to begin playing out.

First Miracle – Angels

I felt my whole back become warm. I thought my friends had come to offer me comfort and put their hands on me with consoling words of prayer. I opened my eyes and expected to see people.

What I saw was an angel on his knees all crouched down. I could feel the power of God from this angel. He wore a tan tunic with a crude belt and sandals and he had the most strikingly beautiful, reddish brown hair that hung down past his shoulders in waves. The angel was majestic as I would have imagined.

And there appeared an angel to him from heaven,
strengthening him. (Luke 22:43)

He was facing forward and he had his head nestled in the crook of my neck on the right side though I didn't feel much sensation. He appeared to be extremely tall as he sat on his knees and hunched over quite a bit to finish his mission. A strong thought came to me that he was doing something to make sure the tumor wouldn't burst. I decided to be reverent and let him finish, so I closed my eyes with my hands folded and waited.

Bless the Lord, you His angels, who excel in strength,
who do His word, heeding the voice of His word.
(Psalms 103:20)

Another minute went by as I could feel more eyes staring at me to my left. Barely opening my eyes, another angel was sitting on his knees about eight feet away on the floor facing me. While staring at me, he had a basket on his lap not appearing as tall or mighty as the one to my right. He sat with no emotion holding the basket as if this was his only task.

This angel had a darker, greenish/brown tunic with a belt and sandals. His wavy, brown hair was shorter than the first angel and when our eyes met, he didn't change his solemn expression. Again, in reverence, I closed my eyes and folded my hands waiting for the heavenly angels to finish their task.

A minute later, I sensed hundreds of eyes staring from the front. I opened my eyes and saw a sea of angels standing before me. They were shorter and seemed to be almost a different species from the first two and only observing as if to learn from this encounter. Their heads were like the waves of the ocean with each row visible and semi-symmetrical. Some rows had blended in with others behind them. I don't know what part they played, but I closed my eyes and folded my hands as I waited for them to finish too.

Satin, a friend from church came over a few minutes later and asked me if I was doing all right. I was so emotionally moved by the fact that God sent angels to help me. I wanted to explain about the angels, but I burst into tears. I was sobbing so hard that Satin couldn't understand me. I felt so honored and I was thrilled to have seen into the spiritual realm watching the angels as they helped me stay alive.

God's Health Protocol

Later that Sunday afternoon, under God's direction, I bought special plant-based vitamins through another friend. The vitamins and the water were to help bring my body into a state of homeostasis, allowing my body to heal naturally. My friend educated me about eating dark green, leafy vegetables which would also aid my body to heal itself naturally. The water machine and the plant-based nutrients have been around for decades.

I figured a hundred million other people used this plan to get healthy from serious life threatening conditions before me. Since then, I've seen this same protocol work on so many big health issues and keep others healthy as well.

Family Arrived

That evening I cleaned the house, cooked the food, shopped and did all the usual things you'd do for visiting family. My family arrived on Monday morning just a few days after my grave diagnosis. I had lost thirty-five pounds and a gray hue was evident to my pasty white skin color. As I greeted everyone, they were unable to hide their shocked and frightened faces as I did look close to death.

Duane and Frank asked at different times if God had told me I would live. I had to tell them both no, but explained how it all added up that I would not only survive, but thrive. I had unfulfilled prophecies. The Spirit told me to buy the water machine and the nutritional products. I told them each that I didn't need God to tell me as I had done the math and had faith for the rest.

Over the next several days, I would occasionally go into the kitchen and find a family member crying with someone else giving them a consoling hug.

I'd honestly be surprised and would genuinely ask, "What's wrong?"

They'd harshly respond, "You know!"

"Oops! Sorry, I forgot," I'd tell them as I tiptoed quietly away.

I genuinely did forget about the cancer. The family was suffering, but I was not. God and I shared a secret that I would quickly be healed. This would reveal to all my family that God was real and in control of my dire health circumstance. I was anxious for my next CAT scan knowing it would report that I was completely healed. How I wished I could break off a little piece of my faith and give it to my three children and my brother!

I announced to the rest of our family and all our friends that I was dying of cancer. I made these wild, outlandish claims about God who had already given me a recipe to heal naturally and I would live. Everyone could hear the passion in my voice that I believed what I told them, but nobody believed me. I had so many eyes on me over the next several months as they were all watching and waiting to see what would happen.

Three weeks after the original diagnosis, I heard God tell me in a calm and nonchalant tone, "Okay, you can have the operation."

By the Spirit's voice, I knew things would go well and I wasn't worried, but I covered all aspects of my life and the operations with prayer. Doing so was my responsibility.

Second Miracle – I'm still Alive

I spoke to the doctor. He said it was a miracle I was still alive. Tumors like mine usually keep growing while filling with blood then explode like a water balloon before they get this big. He said he was happy to help me and we scheduled the surgery two days later.

―――――⊶∘⟨⟨⟨∞⟩⟩⟩∘⊶―――――

This was the confirmation I had been waiting for over the weeks. I heard the doctor and felt a check in my spirit as I realized the angels at church did stop the growth of the tumor and kept it from bursting open inside me.

―――――⊶∘⟨⟨⟨∞⟩⟩⟩∘⊶―――――

I can do all things through him (Jesus) who strengthens me.
(Philippians 4:13)

Ask Yourself...

- *How have others reacted around me when I have truly stood in faith?*
- *How much of God's plan did He reveal to me at the time of my test?*
- *How did this help me to stand in faith through that trial in my life?*
- *Am I stronger for going through this tough time?*
- *Am I less afraid of these trials now that I've proven to myself I can be successful?*

-23-

Cancer Surgeries

I knew that a single mistake by the doctor's scalpel could cause something catastrophic to happen. With great faith I prayed and believed that the Lord would send angels to protect me and guide the surgeon's scalpel.

Third Miracle

I was to have two procedures. The first was to cauterize the veins which fed the tumor. They gave me an intravenous anesthesia. I was awake through the whole procedure. The doctor and the other medical professionals were talking and laughing with each other while operating thinking I was anesthetized. I enjoyed listening to all their stories about their families, going camping and teaching their children to ride bikes.

I had my eyes shut and was holding still. The doctor told the staff he was halfway done and I opened my eyes and saw the doctor lift up to stretch his back muscles and asked, "Am I still supposed to be awake?"

Everyone gasped and asked me how long I had been awake. I told them I had been awake the whole time.

"That's impossible, you never moved!" they all said.

I started recalling all their stories with the exact details of their conversations. Soon they stopped me, believing I had been awake. There were about four of them in the room and they started to question if they should continue since they couldn't give me any more anesthesia.

Since I hadn't flinched yet and felt fine, I asked them to proceed. I also reminded them they were halfway done and stopping might kill me. They said they weren't sure of the legal ramifications.

Smiling, I raised my eyebrows as I said, "I won't tell if you won't." Oops, I just told!

They nervously talked this situation over and the only conclusion was to proceed. Nobody talked. They tried not to keep looking at me, but it was difficult for them. This great medical team was worried. The doctor performing the cauterization procedure told me to hold completely still.

"Like I have been?" I said confidently.

The team continued as time dragged on as the fun stories stopped. Finally, they were done.

The Kidney and Tumor Operation

I was wheeled into the next operating room. My doctor was waiting to remove my dead left kidney and the tumor. The doctor and staff didn't know I was still awake as I had my eyes closed as the hall ceiling lights were flickering and bothering me.

They flung the sheet off and four people instantly grabbed my arms and legs and threw me on the next operating table.

In the middle of this I yelled, "Hey, be careful! That's not nice, I'm naked!"

After I was moved, they covered me with a sheet again. Everyone in the operating room watched me. I glanced at my surgeon and confidently gave him a little smile.

He asked me why I wasn't out and I told them, "I haven't been knocked out yet, but the last group certainly tried. Have fun and good luck!"

The anesthesiologist put a mask on me and I was out in five seconds. The operation was successful.

Forth Miracle

The nurse woke me later and I was instantly awake. They said I did miraculously well. I was bypassing the critical care unit and the drain tubes and was headed for a regular hospital bed.

As I was wheeled down the hall headed for my room, I could see Bernie and two of my children, Duane and Alicia, at the end of the hall in the waiting area.

Excited, I yelled, "Hey everybody, I'm not going to the critical care unit at all! I'm doing much better than expected, so I get a regular bed!"

I beamed and gave them two thumbs up as I rolled by. I could see the relief on their faces. With big smiles they gave me the thumbs up too.

Fifth Miracle

As I was being wheeled down the hall, a door with no handle on the hall side opened.

One of my operating nurses leaned out and yelled, "Congratulations miracle patient!"

I said, "Hey, thank you," not really knowing what she meant, but expecting God's miracles through this whole experience.

In preparation for this operation, Alicia asked her friends and pastors to each write a healing scripture of their choice on an index card. Alicia taped them on the walls of my hospital room. Anyone who came in would see them and read them either out loud or whisper to themselves. It was a brilliant idea to turn those scriptures into prayers and declarations.

Early the next morning, my surgeon came in, sat down and put his elbows on his knees with his face in his hands. His face was pale and extremely distressed as he peered up at me from a bent over posture.

He said, "It's impossible, but the adrenal gland on the dead kidney was still one hundred percent perfect according to pathology. I removed it as I had to. I don't know what to say. Forgive me, I'm so sorry!"

Bernie and I stared at each other as we laughed, still expecting miracles. The doctor appeared confused and said, "I'm so sorry. I don't know if this has ever happened before. This is medically impossible!"

I laughed and pointed to Heaven saying, "You removed a viable organ? That's okay, I forgive you. God's in control anyway and He's going to have it His way!"

The doctor couldn't help but pay attention as we told him about God's hand in my life. A live organ cannot sustain life attached to a dead one. In this case, the kidney had been dead for nine months. The adrenal gland living on top of it was still very much alive. Only God can do this, right?

I elbowed Bernie and we laughed again in delight. The doctor watched us in utter confusion. I was hoping he was re-evaluating his beliefs about God. He was witnessing all God's blessed results and we were expecting more.

Sixth Miracle

Then the doctor said, "I looked around inside when I opened you up and I couldn't see any cancer at all, anywhere. Everything else looked perfect, even your liver."

We weren't surprised and were giving God the glory through our laughing, raising our hands and thanking Jesus out loud as the doctor watched. The doctor sized us up wondering what secrets Bernie and I had that he wasn't privy to.

The next morning I felt great, so I asked the nurse, "What do I have to do to go home?"

The nurse said, "You have to eat, drink, go to the bathroom and walk."

I thought about it and decided to work on the list. Rolling my IV drip stand along with me I walked to the bathroom and back again. I had no problem. I sat down to rest for a few minutes. Then I rolled my IV stand down the hall and back again.

This seemed to work fine. The nurses screamed when they saw me walking and rushed over to me with hands ready to catch me when I fell – not if I fell, but when I fell. I was a little weak, but I definitely had enough strength to walk.

Seventh Miracle

The nurses told me, "This is impossible and you need to go back to bed."

I thought they were joking, so I continued my hike down the hall to build up my strength and endurance. I had four nurses walking on all sides of me with their hands out ready to catch me. I walked five minutes total and went back to bed to rest. An hour later, I walked seventy-five feet and back again. Then I walked the whole three hundred foot loop around the hospital floor.

I kept track and did this ten times. Half way through the day, the nurses stopped following me. They were still shaking their heads every time I passed by.

They asked me, "Please say hello to us when you pass by, so we don't worry or try to find you."

I checked in every time I walked the loop and before I went back to bed. They'd make some kind of joke that they didn't have time to follow me anymore. I joked back telling them I didn't need them as much as those other sick people.

The next day I walked the whole floor a total of thirty times. I was ready to go home. I completed the list of items required of me. They wouldn't let me out yet.

On the third day, I walked around the floor another thirty times and became insistent I could go home since I functioned fine. I did this all before ten o'clock in the morning. Determined to build up my strength through walking the halls, the hospital seemed more like a gym than a hospital. Finally, the nurse said another doctor was coming who needed to release me. I walked a few more rounds before heading to my room.

The head doctor of the hospital, a few other doctors and many interns were crammed in my hospital room. They were all smiling and waiting for me as I walked into my room. I was surprised. I scanned the room and saw my doctor sitting down off to the side at the back of the room. He was watching, his face pale with his forehead resting on his hands and his elbows on his knees. He was shaking his head. I prayed he was still re-evaluating his belief concerning God.

Kicking my tennis shoes off, I bounced into bed as they all watched. The head doctor greeted me warmly stating he wanted to meet me in person and release me himself as he'd heard miraculous reports. The other doctors and interns were all watching and smiling in amazement. He asked why I was doing so well. I grinned and pointed to Heaven. Everyone smiled and a few nodded their heads in agreement.

The head doctor approached me. "I want to shake the hand of the miracle patient. This is so unbelievable and if I didn't see this firsthand, I wouldn't have believed it."

I told my audience, "God will always have it His way and I owe it all to Him!"

He opened my chart asking me to verify when and what type of surgery was performed on me.

"You have had so many miracles while you've been here! Congratulations! By the way, when we gave you instructions to walk, we meant you should walk to and from the bathroom, not walk all day long around the floor!"

I smirked with a shrug. "Sorry, I didn't understand. Next time you should be more specific."

The head doctor of this large hospital released me, smiling and shaking his head in amazement. I stood and shook his hand with a big grin. My doctor had a hard time watching. He still wasn't happy.

Some believe in coincidences, some believe in their own intelligence and capabilities and some believe in the blessings of God. My doctor believed in his own medical abilities. I'm sure it must have kept that brilliant doctor wide awake at nights constantly wondering how all these miracles kept stacking up.

God loves that doctor as one of His beloved sons and blessed him to be a brilliant and skilled surgeon. He won't forget me and my wild claims that I hear God's voice and that He is always in control. One cannot run from such a mountain of undeniable evidence. The Lord grabbed that doctor's attention and has since piled up more evidence tipping the scales revealing God is alive and well in all our lives. What that brilliant doctor does with this information and evidence is between him and God.

Eighth Miracle

I was checked out on the third day and not the third week and I left the hospital behind me. My house and bed felt so good. I changed my nightgown and laid in bed for ten minutes before I climbed out and walked around the house again.

Ninth Miracle

Other than the surgery to remove the dead left kidney and the six-pound tumor, the doctor reported all the other organs were cancer free without chemo or radiation.

God had already given me three weeks on the water, vitamins and dark, green vegetables which healed all the cancer other than a few spots on the lungs. The tumor and the dead, left kidney needed to be removed. Only after this, the Lord told me to have the operation.

Tenth Miracle – The Best One

A half hour after I arrived home from the hospital, I called Mom to tell her I was home. Before she picked up the phone, she looked at the caller ID. Her heart sank as she answered praying it wasn't Bernie with bad news. She was confused when I spoke. Mom had been a medical transcriptionist for twenty five years and knew this was one of the biggest operations a person could have. I was out of the hospital in three days, not three weeks.

Mom asked, "Are you home?"

"Yes, I am!"

Excitedly, she screamed, "There is a God, there is a God!"

I asked, "Do you want to take the next step?"

"Yes, of course I do!"

As I prayed, she repeated a prayer of salvation. A second or two into her prayer, I heard a scuffle out in the living room. Our guests were arguing, pushing and cursing which was totally out of character for them both.

A thought came to mind that the enemy, the devil, was creating a clever diversion. He hoped to stop Mom from giving her life to Jesus. The devil had Mom's eternity in his hands all her life and he was determined to keep her there. He understood that if Mom completed her prayer she was going to Heaven. I was upset, but also understood the enemy was using my guests as a crafty interruption at the most important moment in Mom's life.

I stuck my finger in my ear to block the noise and continued peacefully with the prayer until she finished with the *amen*.

The enemy was defeated as Mom became a child of God and would be a citizen of Heaven after she left this earth. Jesus became Mom's Lord and Savior!

After the prayer, I walked out to see what was happening. The argument was over, though some hard feelings lasted for a few years.

Mom was a changed woman from that moment on. At eighty-two Mom became a believer. The Spirit taught her so much and she became a seasoned believer within a few months.

He forgives all my sins and heals all my diseases.
(Psalms 103:3)

God showed me how to bring my body into a state of homeostasis to allow the healing to take place. The Lord expects me to pass that information along to many others which I have. Many people are living healthy lives because of that gift from God. I passed it along and they passed it along and God's blessings keep multiplying.

The doctors called my healing a spontaneous remission. I call the healings a blessing of a divine nature as the Spirit of the Lord spoke to me giving me the cancer answer even before the problem showed up. A mere three weeks later, all the cancer was healed except a little in my lungs. I had to work a little harder and longer to get healthy.

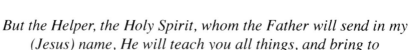

I will take these products for the rest of my life and if I eat well and keep my stress level low, I expect to live a long and healthy life. God can and does use many different ways to heal us. This time He used some old fashioned, healthy lifestyle changes, the best nutritional supplements, great water and eating more raw, green leafy vegetables. Oh, let's not forget to exercise, at least walking every day.

But the Helper, the Holy Spirit, whom the Father will send in my (Jesus) name, He will teach you all things, and bring to your remembrance all things that I said to you.
(John 14:26)

Ask Yourself...

- *Has God given me a gift He wants me to share with others?*
- *How can I be obedient and do this often and with success?*
- *Who do I know that needs to hear my testimony?*
- *Am I willing to step out in faith and share my testimony?*

-24-

Transplanted Kidney

Six months later, I was enjoying the fellowship at church, laughing and chatting after our church service. Erin kept watching me. She is my age and is a wonderful, prophetic woman. Her eyes were nervously following my every move and I noticed. A warm flush crept across her face with embarrassment. She tried to cover it up by giving me a fake smile, but only produced an odd expression. She couldn't hide her behavior as she realized I knew something was up. She and I recently became more than acquaintances as we had been getting to know each other on a more personal level.

I walked straight toward her. She glanced around and fidgeted as she ran her fingernails up and down the seam of her purse strap. She knew it was time to tell me what was on her mind. Half joking, I stood in front of her invading her personal space and smiled.

"What's going on, Erin?"

"Joni," she said in a weakened voice, "I am so embarrassed to tell you this crazy thing that came to me. It certainly appears to be from the Spirit, but it doesn't make any sense at all. I don't have any peace about keeping it to myself, so here it is. God keeps telling me to tell you that you have a transplanted kidney...and it's in the water."

My head jolted back in astonishment as I laughed out loud while telling her, "Erin! It makes perfect sense to me!"

"What?" She said leaning forward in disbelief as she replied, "Well, tell me all the details because I don't understand it at all!"

Erin and I spent ten minutes together as I shared and filled her in on most of the details surrounding the miracles of the cancer experience. She loved hearing my testimony and I loved sharing it all with her!

For prophecy never came by the will of man, but holy men of God spoke as they were moved by the Spirit.
(2 Peter 1:21)

Ask Yourself...

- *Am I being obedient to share what God shows to me even if I don't understand?*
- *What have I learned from reading the author's story about sharing what God has given me?*
- *Does this testimony give me the confidence to step out even when I am unsure?*
- *Will I find my boldness and speak what I hear or see?*
- *What is the importance of following through in the now?*

Section Four:

God Stories

In the same way, let your light shine before others,
so that they may see your good works and give glory to your
Father who is in Heaven.
(Matthew 5:16)

-25-

Clean Fridge

Over the years I had become quite picky about which students I would allow to move into our home. Having kicked out seven students in seven years for various bad behaviors, I pretty much learned to be discerning. Bernie and I were hosting international students attending English immersion schools in Portland. I had an open room that I wanted to fill. There were more students than available housing in my area, so I felt fortunate to have my pick. I've always prayed over my house and my students daily as I want us all to be happy living together.

> *Therefore I tell you, whatever you ask in prayer,*
> *believe that you have received it, and it will be yours.*
> (Mark 11:24)

A nice young man and I were emailing back and forth and he made an appointment to visit our home that day. I cleaned the house, going about my usual routine until I was satisfied with my job. I walked toward my office to do some work.

On the way down the hall, I heard the Spirit tell me, "Clean the refrigerator."

I thought this was an odd statement coming from God. Making an about face, I took a few extra few minutes to throw out a few leftovers, lined containers along the sides and wiped the glass shelves. The refrigerator sparkled again in three minutes. I took another few minutes and cleaned out the student refrigerator too.

I felt God urge me, "Freshen up the sink with bleach," which I did.

Fifteen minutes later, a nice young man arrived with two friends. One of his friends had lived in the United States for three years and claimed to understand Americans well.

I was giving my usual tour of the house. We ended up in the kitchen. One the three men asked, "Can I look in your refrigerator? I know it's an odd request, but it's important, okay?"

"Yes," I said in surprise.

Realizing God positioned me in a place of honor with these young men, I watched as they crowded each other, bent over inspecting the contents of my refrigerator. At first glance, they laughed exclaiming they were amazed at my fridge.

"Americans don't clean their refrigerators. We were laughing on the way over here that the first house with a clean refrigerator would be the house we chose. That is, if we could find a clean one at all!"

They walked over together, peering down to examine the perfectly clean, white sink.

They laughed again, remarking, "Americans don't clean their sinks either, but yours is perfect!"

Later, I realized that while these three men were driving to my house laughing about Americans not cleaning their refrigerators or sinks, the Lord was urging me to clean mine.

Simply placing the desire in that young man's heart to live in my home wasn't enough. God took it a step further setting the stage for all three to pick my house, making it perfectly obvious that the Lord set this up as another blessing. I was grateful as this young man stayed with us eight months and he was a great man.

Until that moment, I realized I had chalked up my success to hard work, being lucky, sometimes to coincidence and lastly, to God. My lack of gratitude gave me pause to re-evaluate my attitude toward our amazing God. It dawned on me later that afternoon that God has nothing but patience, grace and more gifts for me even through my less-than-stellar attitude toward Him.

—◦◦◦—

I was certainly surprised to hear God ask me to clean my refrigerator and the sink that day. I was delighted at the end results knowing God set it up for me to present my best side to those men. Shouldn't I be doing the same by praising His name and glorifying Jesus in the eyes of others?

God was demonstrating that He listens and responds to our prayer requests. We owe it all to Him as every breath we take is a blessing. Bring Jesus with you everywhere you go and be open about your relationship in regards to following Him.

It's hard to retrain ourselves to go against the world's belief system of coincidence and good old-fashioned elbow grease. I have been a bit lazy when it comes to working on my faith in God. I want to dig deeper spending more time each day in quiet rest waiting upon the Lord.

—◦◦◦—

And whatever we ask we receive from him, because we keep his commandments and do what pleases him.
(1 John 3:22)

Ask Yourself…

- *If I dig deep enough will I find I believe a mixture of coincidence, luck, my own efforts and lastly, God's hand in my life?*
- *What do I believe about my faith after reading this short testimony?*
- *Am I aware that the Lord constantly sets the stage allowing us to present ourselves in the best light?*
- *Shouldn't I be doing the same for Him?*
- *What changes can I make to accomplish this goal?*

-26-

Decree a Thing

Bernie and I were searching for a home to buy. We were in constant prayer that the Lord would lead us to the right one. We couldn't afford a fixer-upper nor did we want one. I kept having a strong urge from the Lord that He had this particular one in mind for us. I didn't have concrete evidence from Him yet.

Bernie and I loved hosting international students who attend one of the local English immersion schools in our area. We needed a home with enough bedrooms and bathrooms enabling us to give them the most comfortable home.

We loved this house as soon as we walked around it, but it had too many issues. We questioned if this was the right house for us. It wasn't in the best neighborhood and the inside needed to be updated, painted and it needed new carpet, another bathroom and a few more bedrooms.

This house would work well as Bernie could remodel it without it costing too much. We both saw the potential of a few more bedrooms and a bathroom if we converted the family room.

We loved the three quarter acre, fenced yard which gave us all the privacy we had longed for in the past. Bamboo and other exotic trees and bushes grew in the beautiful woods of the backyard. It was totally private and had a great patio. It even had a little waterfall which helped create a peaceful atmosphere. Beyond that was the official entrance to the woods with paths here and there.

If we lived here we would have the best of both worlds. We could have privacy and country living with the benefit of living a five minute walk to the train that could take our students directly downtown. Bernie and I both sighed when we heard birds chirping as we checked the yard and the woods. It felt like a little oasis in the middle of town.

However, the downside of buying this house was huge! The house to the left was in terrible shape. Black garbage bags lay in mounds around the yard, joined by messy piles of junk. Four dogs guarded this messy house and barked all the time. The yard smelled from the street with all the doggie doo-doo.

The house behind us was vacant and the weeds were three feet high. It had boarded up windows and doors, but there was evidence of a new homeless camp by the filth and junk piling up.

The property across the street was a field of blackberry bushes about ten feet tall. We saw the leftovers of a poorly cleaned dump site.

Across the street from the train stop where my students would wait, there were many sketchy people who hung out. Some of these people were extremely scary. Many of them acted strange and I felt that they might be dangerous.

This house sat on a dirt road and had a community mailbox a block away. The dirt potholes were sometimes a foot deep and were often filled with mud. I prayed about this house and still felt a strong sense it was the one for us.

After we made an offer on the house, I called my friend and pastor, Patti, for her advice. She is full of godly wisdom and I wanted her opinion. I know she has my back and I needed a second pair of godly eyes on our dilemma.

Patti told me they wouldn't come over to see the house as it wasn't necessary. Being a little hurt by her words she further explained what she meant.

"Since you have the Spirit inside of you, you change the atmosphere wherever you go. If you want the house, then the neighborhood will improve to your standards because of your presence. Don't forget to pray and decree what changes you would like to see."

Wow, I was excited to hear that statement. My faith was strong after hearing this and I had total peace about moving forward. I chose to declare over the neighborhood for three blocks away in all directions, all the way to the train station and all the way to downtown.

We could afford this house and it had possibilities. Our realtor said no other offers had been made in the two years it had been on the market. I believe God's hand was over this property as it sat waiting for us to be in a position to buy it. We put our faith on the line and bought this questionable fixer upper.

The First Change

After we bought the house, the city building commission changed their rules. They have since been willing to bend the rules to the point of breaking them in order to have more houses built for the tax revenue. This will increase the value of the property as many townhomes can be built on the back of the property.

The Second Change

We found out the reason so many sketchy people were hanging out at the train stop. There was a methadone clinic across the street from the train station. This clinic suddenly closed even before we moved into our house which drastically changed the atmosphere of the train station.

The Third Change

The house next to us was sold to a man who remodeled it inside and out. It became quite beautiful with expensive bamboo flooring, granite countertops, expensive trim and new everything, inside and out. We now have wonderful neighbors who are great people and our friends.

The Fourth Change

The fourth change was that homeless camp behind us was cleaned up.

The Fifth Change

The owner of the property with the homeless camp hired someone to bulldoze everything off the property. It took two weeks to level the house, the outbuilding, the trees, the shrubs and to haul it all away. The owner said he was splitting the property and would be building big beautiful townhomes next door soon. Roads are being built on the property and we see pink flags staked here and there, so we know new houses are right around the corner.

The Sixth Change

I drove out of my driveway one day and talked to a nice man who was surveying the blackberry bushes across the street. He was the owner and planned to develop the property by building nice big houses. We see the beginnings of a development.

The Seventh Change

The next change was that the three little houses on the other side of the street will be fixed up and sold. One has already been beautifully remodeled. I can image the others will be fixed up nicely as well.

The Eighth Change

Another change was to the house on the other side of our driveway. The owner was taking and selling drugs and allowed a homeless man to stack his garbage on the sides of the house and in the back yard. I could hear fighting in the middle of the night and called the police many times to stop the violence.

It was recently vacated due to foreclosure and the bank has cleaned up the house completely. It's now sold to a nice family. Now all the houses on that street have friendly owners who take care of their homes and are very nice people.

My daughter, Natalie, and I were talking on the phone. She was telling me how Bernie and I are the perfect people to host international students and that our house is great for hosting. She was listing all the reasons why and I was listening with a big smile as I soaked up the compliments.

In the middle of what Natalie was saying, I heard the Spirit of the Lord say, "Yes, that's why I put you here in this house!"

Thank You, Lord, for once again reminding me that it is always You!

The Ninth Change

We woke up recently hearing the rumblings of heavy equipment being used close by. I walked down our driveway and saw a big crew of men paving the road in front of our house. Some of the other neighbors got together and paid for our new road telling me they were tired of the dust and potholes.

The Tenth Change

A year ago, I heard the Spirit ask me to remodel three of our eight bedrooms and a bathroom at the far side of our house. He wanted us to remodel it into an apartment for our friends/pastors. They stayed with us for almost a year before the Spirit told me it was the appointed time for them to move out.

At that same time, God directed Bernie and me to remodel the rest of the house and put it on the market.

We have been working non-stop and with the help of my daughter, Natalie, and her family we are turning our worn-out 1977 home into a beautiful house ready to sell.

Natalie, Dani, Titus and Monica moved in recently as they sold their house and are looking to buy their next in a specific area.

With all the extra space, we have plenty of room to stretch out. All of us are grateful to have the apartment that God provided.

Recently, I heard the Spirit ask me, "Who would want to buy an eight bedroom, three bath house?"

I answered out loud with a little chuckle, "Probably nobody!"

The Spirit asked me, "Then who would want to buy a five bedroom, two bath house with a separate apartment ready to rent for extra income to pay the mortgage?"

Laughingly, I responded, "Wouldn't everyone?"

The Spirit responded, "That's why I asked you to turn the back bedrooms and bathroom into a one bedroom apartment last year. I wanted to bless Rich and Patti last year, you and Bernie now with the extra room for the kids and bless you with a great house to sell. If I would have asked you to build an apartment and remodel the whole house now you would have been overwhelmed. Now it's less of a task. The house is worth much more and doesn't seem like such a huge job now."

On the verge of tears, I felt so loved and blessed by God. I nodded my head in awe from that brief conversation with the Spirit of God. Like most people, God had to explain all the moving parts of our blessings. I might not have ever noticed or added it all up by myself. In light of all this, it makes sense to give thanks to God in all things now, doesn't it?

Bernie and I didn't have much more than five hundred dollars to remodel the whole house. We have waited upon the Lord for Kingdom finances and it came flooding in through Bernie's work. He never made so much money in his life.

We will sell our house in a few months and build a smaller home. There are houses being built on the property behind us and our real estate agent said that will raise the value of our house. Bernie is set to retire after the sale of our home. Thank you, Father, Jesus and Holy Spirit!

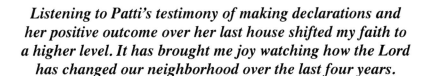

Listening to Patti's testimony of making declarations and her positive outcome over her last house shifted my faith to a higher level. It has brought me joy watching how the Lord has changed our neighborhood over the last four years.

…decree a thing and it shall be established… (Job 22:28 ASV)

Ask Yourself...

- *Will I ask in prayer decreeing what changes I want and believe to receive?*
- *Can I establish this as a habit and pay attention to what God is telling me?*
- *In what areas will I decree a change?*
- *Am I aware that my decrees have to line up with the word of God?*
- *Will I start decreeing a change today using other scriptures to back up my plan?*

-27-

Flame Jumper

The Lord gave me a prophetic vision one morning while I was praying. It was a warning of what was to come. I was standing on some kind of a landing with a white backdrop. To my left was a staircase leading to Heaven. Some of the stairs were beautiful and easy to climb, but a few stairs were steep and angled poorly posing a challenge to those who made a choice to walk the narrow path of love, grace and truth. Some of these stairs were old and unsafe while others were beautifully built, seemingly from marble. This mixture of steps, both safe and treacherous, stretched upwards into the clouds.

To my right, I saw a small ledge jutting out over a burning pit lit by beautiful golden and bronze flames rising from below. From the wear and tear along its well-worn ledge consisting of fine dust and small pebbles, this pit had many visitors. Unfortunately, this was a familiar place I had visited too many times in my life. I glanced at the staircase, but my curiosity got the better of me. I was strangely drawn to investigate the flickering flames a little below the ledge. What bothered me in that moment was that I was more interested in the fiery pit than I was in the heavenly staircase.

A few seconds later, I found myself standing in the middle with the staircase to my left and the ledge of flames to my right as if I was making a personal choice for myself. I turned to my right. The mystery of the flames rising high was enticing me and I wanted to know more. I slowly moved little by little, scuffing my clean, white tennis shoes in the dust while craning my neck to peek down into the flames. I wanted to inch closer to see over the ledge though I had to be careful not to give myself completely over to the pit as I was just an observer and not a participant this time. Dirt billowed in the air as I inched closer.

While the flames made my spirit uneasy, these golden and bronze flames warmed me and I felt somewhat comforted and attracted to this familiar spot. It seemed pleasant enough to be at the ledge and I only felt a twinge of guilt, though just being there I was still giving into rebellion. It was not a good place to be.

I still moved forward as I knew better than to be lulled into this false sense of peace. I spent too long standing on the ledge peering over. I couldn't see the bottom, but I had a sense it wasn't too far down and this flaming pit didn't seem all that dangerous.

In my spirit, I knew this was a trap to ensnare those of us who are just too tired, lazy or upset to work at keeping our words in check, to be kind to one another.

I understood this was a place for people to make choices, usually bad choices. The flames and the fire didn't seem as terrible as you'd expect, but that was the deception of it all. I had the idea that once you came here then you would be back again and again, justifying your actions and subtly lowering your standards of godly behavior.

Out of the same mouth come blessing and cursing.
My brothers, these things should not be this way. (James 3:10)

This pit has many names. This pit is a place where the struggle between working at being loving and kind versus allowing ourselves to be careless in word and deed takes place in our hearts.

This pit is offered to us every day by the enemy of our soul. The enemy tries to convince us we can give in just for this one situation, just this one time and just for now... really, it's no big deal! This attitude comes served up with a heaping, steaming plate of rebellion and two side orders of deceit and lies and will take us down the road to other bad habits which will be hard to break.

Suddenly, I found myself thirty feet away, an equal distance from both the staircase and the flaming pit. Someone was standing where I had been. This person hardly even gave the staircase a second glance.

This person walked boldly up to the edge of the flaming pit, peered over and without a second thought said, "Ah, whatever!" Then he backed up to get a running start and threw himself screaming and laughing into the flames. He flung himself in a wildly, rebellious flip through the air as he freely dove right in. I could see his hair waving in the wind, catching in drafts of heat as he fell. This person didn't want to work at being godly at this moment, but instead took the immediate and easy route. When we rebelliously jump into the flaming pit it becomes easier and deeper and so does our sinful nature. This was the end of the vision.

A few hours later, this same person called me on the phone and wanted to pick a fight with me. I stopped the call as soon as I realized my vision was a warning from the Lord and the conversation was going nowhere.

———————<<<≪≫>>>———————

In the past, I would have tried to convince this person to my way of thinking, staying on the phone in anguish. If I hadn't been warned from the Spirit, I might have been devastated for the whole day nursing my hurt feelings and possibly talking about it. It was difficult for a few minutes, but I had this vision fresh in my mind and composed myself quickly not allowing myself to get sucked into an argument and being upset. I was so grateful for this godly vision.

Life can be difficult at times. We all extend grace to others because we know they are sometimes having an "Ah, whatever!" moment of weakness. We all struggle with this issue at one time or another. However, it is our choice to be pulled into these situations and allow ourselves to be emotionally battered.

———————<<<≪≫>>>———————

God knew I needed correction in this area. I don't allow people to pull me into their drama when they are choosing a bad attitude and want to take it out on me. I simply get off the phone or walk away wishing them well with a smile and never mention it again. This is my way of extending grace to others.

The tongue is a fire, a world of iniquity. The tongue is so set among our members that it defiles the whole body and sets on fire the course of nature, and it is set on fire by hell.
(James 3:6)

Ask Yourself...

- *Am I a flame jumper with habits of being lazy and careless in word and deed?*
- *Will I choose today to guard my tongue and watch my attitude to convey wisdom and kindness?*
- *Can I remember a time when I was a flame jumper?*
- *What were the circumstances and how did I feel about myself and the episode later?*
- *Am I aware that I can ask God to help me control my tongue and my attitude each day knowing He is happy to help me? Am I willing to do so?*

-28-

Annie's Story

Annie was a saint. She was easy to love and we all did. She and I were instant friends when we first met at the Christian singles group at a local church when I was in my late forties. We always had so much fun, kept each other honest and prayed for one another.

We were friends for about ten years. She was the one who organized the dance lessons where my husband's Christian singles group and ours met once a week. This is where Bernie and I first met and fell in love.

Both of us eventually married and surprisingly, we lived only about five minutes apart from each another. Annie married Rob who said he was the luckiest man on earth. We enjoyed a couples' Bible study once a week with several other couples.

She and Rob had only been married a few years when they made plans to go to Mexico for a vacation with another couple.

Warning–Trip to Mexico

After I heard of her plans, the Spirit prompted me to warn her, "Annie, God just told me to tell you something. Don't go to Mexico. It won't end well for you."

For it is not you who will be speaking, it will be the Spirit of your Father speaking through you. (Matthew 10:20)

After I spoke, she quickly averted her eyes from mine making me believe she heard the Spirit's truth in my words. She tried to assure me she would be fine and told me not to worry.

I tried to be helpful by suggesting they go to Hawaii instead, but her excuse was the four of them had already made up their minds. I've been to both places many times and thought they could easily change their destination and still have a great time. Annie had never been to Mexico, but she vacationed in Hawaii once.

A few days later, the Spirit told me to tell her a second time, "Annie, God told me again to tell you please don't go to Mexico. It won't end well for you."

Annie became angry at me and turned her head to face me with a glare.

"I told you, we're still going and we'll all be fine! Don't tell me again!"

A week later, the Spirit prompted me for the third time to urge her not to go to Mexico.

"Annie, God told me to tell..." my voice trailed off as she interrupted me.

"Stop it, Joni, no more! I'm not talking about this with you again!"

The Spirit quietly and gently said, "Don't say another word about the trip or the warning."

I did worry about her as I wondered what harm God was trying to keep her from while in Mexico.

Giving her these warnings from the Spirit changed our relationship. She distanced herself from me somewhat. This is the price I pay for being God's mouthpiece and it has happened to me time and time again. I will be faithful to God over man any day.

...We ought to obey God rather than men. (Acts 5:29)

They vacationed in Mexico with their friends and came back home a few days earlier than planned. The husband of the other couple came home sick from a parasite. He ended up in the hospital and after things settled down, Annie invited me over to her house. She offered me a glass of water while I sat in her living room. I smiled and held the water in my hand while she twirled in the middle of the room laughing with a big smile on her face.

She remarked, "You must have made a mistake. I'm fine! See, nothing's wrong with me. You were wrong about what you thought God told you! The word must have been for our friend!"

Shaking my head, I told her, "No, I wasn't wrong. Annie, I don't understand this, but I know what I heard. You know me! I hear God and you know it too."

Annie had witnessed my prophetic and seer gifts many times.

I asked her, "Are you going to be tested for the parasite too?"

Annie smiled sarcastically and told me, "I'm not sick!"

I needed to let it go and she changed the subject as we began talking about their fun trip. I sat and listened, smiling and pretending this whole thing wasn't upsetting.

Things didn't add up in my mind. Hearing the same word three times loud and clear, I was one hundred percent sure that I heard correctly from God. My word of warning to Annie was so exact, yet seemed like such a mystery to me.

Annie Became Sick

Five months later, she said something was wrong and asked our group of friends to pray about her new health issue. She said the doctor was having some tests done. Annie soon found out she had stomach cancer. We all started scrambling to find a cure for cancer as none of us wanted her to die.

Annie was the glue that held our group together. She and Rob had only been married a short time and this seemed like such a tragedy. We all watched her get sicker as time went by.

While she was sick, I would go to her house for visits and to help out. She would stand up, put her arms up and lace her fingers behind my neck and literally hang on.

She would get close to my ear and whisper quietly, "Joni, ask God for a second chance. Tell God I promise I will listen next time and I am so sorry. I don't want to die."

I didn't quite understand why she was constantly asking me to talk to God on her behalf. My idea was that she knew I was close to God. I never did ask her what she meant by these remarks because they tore me up and brought me to my knees with such sobbing.

We were all praying, but nothing happened as Annie's cancer took its toll on her. We watched her slowly deteriorate for another five months or so. She became weaker and I could barely stand to visit. I would end up crying at the thought of the loss of our wonderful friend. It broke my heart.

Annie died peacefully at home. Her loving family and all of her friends were heartbroken. Her funeral was held at her good friend's house. Many people came to pay their respects. I heard so many stories of her loving kindness.

A few weeks later, Rob admitted to our little group that the doctors diagnosed her with the same parasite from Mexico as their friend contracted and it quickly turned into stomach cancer as it attached itself to her stomach ulcer. She never admitted to me that the word of warning had come true. Perhaps she thought I already knew.

Annie is in Heaven now. God always knew the end result for our dear friend. She has a heavenly perspective now and I'm sure she is having a glorious time and we'll see each other soon enough.

Advice from Heaven

If she could add to this testimony from her heavenly point of view, I'm sure she would tell us to put the Lord first in our lives. Spend time with Him. She would tell us to study and get God's word deep in our hearts and declare all the promises laid out in the Bible. She would tell us to be grateful for all He has given. Annie would tell us to rest in the Lord and listen for Him to speak to us. She would tell us to pray continually, guard our hearts, forgive and don't allow anger and pride to take hold in our lives.

She would tell us to give God all the glory in the big and the small things. Her advice would be to be obedient to God and continually praise Him in the good and bad times. She would tell us to expect to walk in His blessings.

The most important message she would want us to hear is to share the love of Jesus to anyone who will listen and bring as many souls to Heaven as we can.

I had discovered that through sharing Jesus with my family. If I could see everyone around me as potential family, I could share Jesus with them. I could have the faith and the hope that someday, they too would be part of my family – the family of God.

Our dear Annie will surely be missed and spoken about as she has spread the love of Jesus to many people.

It was up to God to confirm the spirit of my prophetic word through the Bible, the Spirit, other people and many other sources. I could see each time I warned her that she turned away and had no peace. Having no peace is a sign something isn't right. Being a strong believer, she sensed going to Mexico was a bad move. She briefly mentioned to me that she hadn't been to Mexico before and it was too tempting to resist.

We miss our friends and loved ones when they pass away. Believers pass from this life to the next entering Heaven to spend eternity with other saints and God. It must be a beautiful sight to behold every time one of God's children enters Heaven as they experience the greatest love and joy possible. We won't understand until we have made that journey ourselves to see Heaven's splendor!

Annie passed away ten months before the Lord walked me through my cancer answer.

Precious in the sight of the Lord is the death of His saints.
(Psalms 116:15)

Ask Yourself…

- *Have I ever received a warning from a friend and ignored it? How did that work out for me?*
- *Could that friend have been prompted by the Spirit to give me that warning?*
- *Have I ever offered a friend a warning and had them reject it? How did that make me feel?*
- *Did I get hurt and pull back to save the friendship?*
- *What have I learned from this story?*

Section 5:

Let Go…and Let God

My one bit of advice is to tell you to let go…of whatever bad habit or attitude you are holding onto, and let God lead you…by following Him and seeing where he leads you in life. It will be for your good and for God's glory!

Again Jesus spoke to them, saying, "I am the light of the world.
Whoever follows me will not walk in darkness but will have
the light of life." (John 8:12)

-29-

Lucas' Prayers for His Elk

My son-in-law, Lucas, has been working on mastering his hunting skills. He's most of the way there and he recently bought an elk tag hoping to fill their freezer. He had it all planned out in his mind where he'd go and how he'd pack the meat out. He planned on going at the crack of dawn a few mornings before work and thought this was his best plan of action.

Power of Prayer

Lucas knew to pray for provision for his family and he did so before he went hunting early that next morning. He prayed a general prayer to see elk. He saw a big herd of elk, but they were too far away to get a good, clean shot. He came home empty-handed.

Deciding he had to be a little more specific, he prayed they would see a herd of elk closer to where he was in the woods. The next morning they did see a herd of elk that was very close. The problem was there were no bull elks, only cows. He came home empty-handed.

He was catching on and was fired up as he saw how the Lord was blessing him exactly how he prayed. Lucas became more determined and very specific. He prayed to see a herd of elk, close to them with bulls to shoot trusting the next morning he would proudly bag his elk and feed his family for the winter. Lucas was confident in his next hunting trip.

His next trip he saw a large herd of elk close by, but they scattered into the woods quickly, moving too fast and he couldn't get a clean shot. He came home empty-handed.

Lucas went boldly before the Lord in prayer with the help of his wife, my daughter, Alicia. They prayed they would see a herd of elk close to them with a bull to shoot. Together they prayed in detail that an elk of God's choosing would be obedient to His provision for their family. Alicia prayed for a bull elk and one who would not move too much, that it would be dazed and would not keep up with the rest of the herd and be perfectly positioned for a clear shot.

The next morning, Alicia and Lucas went hunting at the crack of dawn and hiked deep in the woods.

Alicia pointed and whispered with excitement, "Look, there's a herd of elk!"

There was a large herd of elk, close to them and they saw two huge bulls standing in front of the others. At first glance, the whole herd reacted as they moseyed into the safety of the woods, except one bull which stood behind the two giant bulls. It stood perfectly positioned in a convenient state of obedience. This average sized bull elk seemed a little dazed and was clearly the one God chose for them.

Lucas shot it in the shoulder and it took a few steps in a semi circle. Lucas took aim again and shot a second time hitting it perfectly in the lungs where it went down. Sweet success! They were excited to fill up the freezer with elk steaks, hamburger and roasts, not to mention jerky. What a blessing for the whole family!

Alicia and Lucas stood there in awe for a moment before praising God with tear-filled eyes knowing in their heart the Lord provided all they desired.

Delight yourself in the Lord,
and he will give you the desires of your heart. (Psalms 37:4)

It took Lucas, their son, Colby, my husband, Bernie, and a few other men many trips to hike two hours in and then two hours out to pack the meat out. Maybe next year they should incorporate into their prayer that the herd of elk would be close to their vehicle too!

Lucas sought God and connected in partnership with confidence that he was praying according to the Lord's will for their lives. He was praying for provision for his family. Lucas will be the first one to admit that the details are important. Praying specifically was part of the Lord's lesson. This testimony reflects how Lucas knew that God heard all his prayers and granted each single request along the way. Lucas and the whole family are greatly blessed by putting God first in their hunting trips as well as all other activities in their lives!

Lucas and Alicia know that God is moved by our faith in Him. They will be the first to proclaim that all problems should be taken to the Lord first. If we need provision for health, finances or anything else we should search scripture on those problems and speak them out loud over our situation. Alicia would recommend that we live our lives with joy, watch and wait to see God solve these problems and give Him praise when we see His results.

And we are confident that he hears us whenever we ask for anything that pleases him. (1 John 5:14)

Ask Yourself…

- *What are the benefits of praying specifically?*
- *Can I see a pattern of blessings when Lucas prayed specifically?*
- *What is the lesson I can learn from this testimony?*
- *What does this story indicate I should start doing?*
- *Will I create a habit to be more specific when I pray?*

-30-

Power of a Testimony

Mom was right. It happened just like she said it would. I did turn into her after all! Sarah shook her head and chuckled to herself as she emptied the kitchen junk drawer onto her beautiful, new granite countertop. She remembered how her Mom trained her and her sister to pick a drawer, closet, or a small bank of cabinets and clean it out each week.

Sarah could hear her Mom now, "If you pick something to deep clean just once a week you won't get behind and it'll only take you ten minutes!"

As soon as the junk drawer was spread out on the counter, she heard the doorbell ring. It was her new neighbor, Leah. Most women would have been embarrassed because she hadn't cleaned the house or taken a shower yet. But she had finished her Bible study for that morning.

It's hard to rattle Sarah as she is one of those people who doesn't take herself seriously. That characteristic is what attracted Leah to Sarah in the first place. Leah was drawn to how she was real and honest and never sugar-coated her words.

Sarah, her husband and their three children moved into their dream house not quite a month before. She was slowly becoming friends with Leah who lived next door. Leah and her husband were not believers and had no children.

Sarah has the spunk and boldness that goes far beyond most other women in their early thirties. Early in any conversation you had with her it would soon be evident she seeks the wisdom of God and doesn't try to hide the fact she loves the Lord. Leah took note of this fact about her new neighbor and was watching how she conducted herself in life. Sarah has the knack of making everyone feel welcome with her warm and charming personality.

With a genuine smile, she invited Leah into her home and offered her some cranberry juice and cut a piece of lemon square for each of them. As the two sat at the kitchen table visiting like long time friends, Leah remarked how she felt comfortable around Sarah. Sarah thanked Leah for the compliment.

She raised her hands off the table about six inches and spoke, "Thank you, Jesus, for my new friend, Leah too!"

Leah asked her what all that religious stuff was about and Sarah was all too happy to tell her. She talked about Jesus and gave her a few testimonies of God's greatness.

A half hour into their talk, Leah confessed she had been wondering about Sarah and God as she'd rarely heard God spoken of in a positive manner. Leah admitted that her angry father taught them God wasn't real. This lesson was usually accompanied with a heavy fist thumped against the table. It was confusing to her because all the ills of the world were also blamed on God. This subject was taboo in her family.

Sarah and Leah talked about their lives until the subject turned to children. Leah suddenly burst into tears and confided in Sarah that she and her husband had been desperately trying to have a baby for years. Nothing happened.

Never one to miss an opportunity, Sarah told her the story of Hannah in the Bible who also wanted a baby. Hannah and her husband had been trying for years to have a child too. Nothing happened. In the middle of all this emotional turmoil, Hannah prayed to God to have a baby. She vowed to give her child back to the Lord all the days of his life.

Finally, God answered her prayer and she became pregnant and gave birth to a son, Samuel. She dedicated her son to the Lord and Samuel became a mighty man of God eventually ruling Israel. There is so much more to this testimony in 1 Samuel.

Being led by the Spirit, Sarah calmly asked her if she could pray over her. Leah agreed. Sarah prayed that God would grant Leah the same favor and that she would have a child too. A half smile came across Sarah's face as her faith never wavered. She continued to speak of the greatness of God as she understood the power of a testimony and explained this godly principle to Leah.

When we share a testimony we offer the blessing to the listener. Sarah explained the listener only needs to reach out in faith and believe to receive a similar blessing.

Leah appeared curious and liked this testimony and said as much. She continued to listen as her heart was touched by all she'd heard, nodding her head occasionally. It was apparent that she was giving serious thought and responded that she never quite heard such a sweet story before. Leah admitted that she hadn't heard much about God her whole life, but her interest was growing.

Staring off in the distant as if really soaking in all she heard, it was obvious to Sarah that Leah had opened her heart to the Lord. Sarah hoped the powerful testimony of Hannah would activate that same blessing in Leah's life too.

Sarah became alert as the Spirit was heavy in the atmosphere. Sarah's smile spread wide across her face and she thought there was a shift taking place in Leah's heart. Their friendship grew and Leah was being drawn in by Sarah's openness in speaking about God.

The two women's friendship continued to flourish. Several months went by before Leah knocked on Sarah's door with a big bouquet of flowers in her hand. Leah explained that something shifted deep inside and her spiritual life changed after Sarah shared Jesus and the story of Hannah and Samuel. Leah was thrilled to report that she was pregnant. Both women squealed with delight and she told Sarah all of this was a miracle knowing God blessed them with a child. Sarah agreed.

Leah recognized God was changing her life and confided that all this was too coincidental. She wanted to learn more about Jesus. Leah happily explained she had been sharing all she learned with her husband. She and her husband soon started attending church with Sarah and her family and became believers!

How did this miracle happen that after Leah heard about how great God was to Hannah that she became pregnant? I believe it was so God could be revealed in her life. This was much like the blind man in the book of John the ninth chapter. Jesus gave him a miracle curing his blindness simply to demonstrate God's love and power.

The following verse in Revelation reveals to us that a testimony of Jesus can open a prophetic window. It activates faith and shifts the impossible into the realm of possibility. Miracles and blessings can flow as we engage with the Lord. It is an invitation for Jesus to do it again!

I (the angel) am a fellow servant with you and your brothers who hold to the testimony of Jesus. Worship God. For the testimony of Jesus is the spirit of prophecy. (Revelation 19:10)

Ask Yourself…

- *Do I believe God has put His Spirit into godly testimonies?*
- *Do I have the faith to believe and declare to see miracles in my life too?*
- *What changes do I want to see?*
- *Am I willing to search and find scriptures and declare them over circumstances?*
- *Will I declare them every day, believe and thank God before I see results?*
- *Will I share my blessings with others to build their faith?*

-31-

Divine Answer

In my early forties, I was awakened in the early morning hours by a phone call. I was delighted that unexpected company was coming for lunch though I only had a few hours to prepare. I took great care in planning the simple menu, mulling over different dishes I could easily serve our group as I rushed to the supermarket.

On the drive, I rolled the window down half way and enjoyed listening to the wind gently blowing the dry leaves of the trees. Rays of early morning light flickered through the swaying trees and into my eyes. I felt great as I enjoyed this unusually warm October day. All was wonderful in my life and I was already having a great day anticipating the enjoyment of a lazy afternoon entertaining and laughing with my friends and family.

There seemed to be only a handful of people scattered throughout the supermarket at that early morning hour. I heard an echo with each step I took. After ten minutes of mindless wandering, I felt satisfied I had gathered all I needed for a great, healthy lunch.

I became preoccupied by planning the day in my mind as I arranged my groceries on the belt at the checkout counter. I suddenly realized the checker was slamming my food into the bag having an obvious tantrum. Holding my breath in disbelief for a moment, I felt a wave of sadness for her.

I heard the Spirit notify me she needed love as she had some big family issues. Through the overflow of God's love, I gently placed my hand on hers which also prevented her from doing any more damage to my food as my bananas and bread still lay on the checkout belt. Without warning, her attitude changed and she lifted her face up at me with surprise.

Not wanting to appear harsh, I asked lovingly, "You're not having a good day today, are you? What's going on with your family?"

Startled by my pointed question, she wondered if I already knew about her circumstances. Her eyes began to well up with tears. She released her emotions and started crying hard and put her hands up to her face to hide her sobbing. I walked around the counter and hugged her. She melted in my arms as her sad story unfolded.

She and her husband recently moved to the area from the next state away. Her baby was sick and the babysitter informed her she was not able to watch her child after that day until her baby was well again. This young mother didn't have family or friends in the area. Her husband was in the hospital and would be there for the next week. She felt desperate and all alone. Tears welled in my eyes as I heard all the heartbreaking details.

During the flurry of her despair and hopelessness, I made the decision to babysit for her. As I opened my mouth to make this offer, the Spirit informed me, "She has a friend who I am sending to help. This friend is already on the way. She will unexpectedly arrive in a few hours."

Slowly, I pulled away and asked if she believed in God. Her only response was that she and her husband began to attend church for the first time a few weeks earlier. She said they loved their new church and had learned so much about the love of God. My heart fluttered with joy as I recognized this was a setup by God, a divine appointment between us. I felt a wave of excitement for her knowing my word from God would unfold and she'd see the hand of God in her life possibly for the first time ever!

I informed her that the Spirit of God just gave me some good news for her. Her eyes became big as she listened to every word about how God had sent an unexpected friend who is already on the way to help. She was stunned, but hopeful. She didn't quite understand, but I recognized that God had His hand in her life solving her problem in her moment of desperation.

She caught her breath and exhaled hard in relief as a effort to stop crying and hoped what I told her was true. She apologized for her rude behavior as she wiped her eyes and blew her nose. She took another deep breath and thanked me for helping her stating she could have lost her job over her poor behavior.

We spoke a few more minutes and she seemed relieved at the good news. I let her know that I would come back early the next morning to find out the details.

I made another trip to the store the next morning. She was thrilled to inform me that a distant cousin did arrive and agreed to stay for a week or more to help her out. She said that all her doubts about God had disappeared. She wouldn't soon forget how God turned her grief into a huge blessing by revealing Himself to her.

We spent a few minutes talking as I began to explain how God sent me to give her encouragement. She interrupted me, happy to tell me that her cousin who arrived the previous afternoon also heard from the Spirit the day before. She made the fourteen-hour drive without calling first which was part of God's plan for that young mother in need. She thanked me for standing with her in grief, hope, then in unexpected joy. We were both overjoyed by seeing God's blessings!

When we step out in faith to speak about God we are taking a step of boldness. We are establishing a closer relationship with the Lord. One success leads to other successes and our faith increases. God is pleased we bring Him into our lives and our problems. In doing so it leads us to have His strength and wisdom.

If I had not spoken what I thought I heard from the Spirit, the impact of that blessing wouldn't have been so great. The store clerk wouldn't have heard about the Lord sending someone to help back up what the distant cousin wanted to reveal about God too.

Ask Yourself...

- *Am I bold enough to speak to strangers on God's behalf when I feel moved by the Spirit to do so?*
- *Do I now see the value in stepping out to speak what I believe the Spirit has asked me to say?*
- *Do I realize that the only ability I need in order to be used by God is my availability to Him?*
- *Am I willing to pray asking to be used by God to accomplish His will?*
- *What will the long-term outcome be if I establish this as a habit?*

-32-

Small and Subtle Mystery

It caught my attention from ten feet away. I raced toward it. I was enthralled at this magnificent piece of art. Its beauty almost took my breath away. I picked it up and felt the cold, glass piece in my hands as I gently wiped the dust off the best I could with my fingers. I examined it as I held it up to the light as the rich, emerald green color glinted ever so slightly in the sunshine beaming through the window.

Its peculiar shape seemed out of character for its purpose. This somewhat quirky piece was crafted with only three legs on which it stood. Mesmerized by its unique beauty, I held it in my hands before I gently turned it on its side to check its price. It was more than I could afford.

Holding it for a few more minutes, I hesitated and resisted the urge to replace it on the dusty shelf. Finally, with a twinge of loss, I set it back down and walked away glancing back at it for a moment as if to say goodbye.

The very next day Mom wandered aimlessly through the store. This same magnificent piece caught her eye. She was enthralled by the same exquisite, emerald green piece. She bought it as a gift, thinking of me.

Mom came over later that day and presented it to me in a small, brown paper bag, folded and crumpled at the top for safety.

As I opened the bag and peered inside, I was both delighted and stunned by what I saw. We talked excitedly for ten minutes as I told her I had my eye on it just the day before. We both wondered how she could have known as we enjoyed and marveled at this amazing story. I found a suitable place of honor for the gift in the middle of my dining room table.

Mom and I remembered and talked about our treasured memory for the rest of her life. This coincidence brought us such pleasure as Mom's attention was drawn to the same green, fifty-cent toothpick holder at the supermarket's priced-to-clear shelves!

I was twenty-years-old at the time and wasn't walking with the Lord. Mom and I marveled at this situation. Still, the question always haunted us as to how Mom knew to buy this piece for me. What drew her attention to this item and why did she think of me as she bought it? This toothpick holder became a symbol of unexplained mystery. We talked about this strange situation as it became a focal point in our conversations and laughter over the years.

In my thirties, I gave my life to Jesus and as a believer I easily recognized God's hand in this gift and I was grateful that He urged Mom to buy it for me. I know God was demonstrating how much He cares about the small and subtle desires of my heart.

After Mom gave her life to Jesus, twenty-five years after I did, the truth became evident to her as we talked about that great memory. Mom finally understood how God arranged this situation shrouded by mystery. The meaning of this small gift changed and it had actually been a blessing from God all along. I began to see it as a symbol of the love I constantly received from Mom as God urged her to buy it for me as a symbol of His love too.

Do to others as you would like them to do to you.
(Luke 6:31)

Ask Yourself...

- *Looking back, can I see that what God has given me is a demonstration of His love?*
- *What was the gift?*
- *Did I understand it was from the Lord?*

-33-

Ambushed!

My Uncle Art was a tough, decorated Green Beret with many metals for bravery for saving the lives of his fellow soldiers. He is one of many true American heroes throughout history.

In the military in the late 1960s, Uncle Art was enjoying a few days off in Thailand. As he walked by a small jewelry shop, something caught his eye in the display window. He stopped and went in out of curiosity.

On display was an impressive tiger claw in a bold, gold setting hanging from a beautiful, thick, gold chain. The salesman explained a tiger claw was thought of as a symbol of protection in Thailand. On a whim, my Uncle Art bought this item for my brother, Frank.

Months later, he presented this uniquely beautiful gift to Frank who was in high school at the time.

Along with the gift came the rather strong, but odd suggestion as Uncle Art said, "You should always wear this around your neck as someday the tiger claw could save your life!"

Uncle Art really didn't know why he made this statement as it just came out of his mouth. Frank did keep the tiger claw around his neck under his shirt ninety-nine percent of the time since that day.

In his fifties, Frank took a trip to Mexico. Frank described this town as being very picturesque and rich with historical architectural value at the base of a beautiful mountain range. Frank would soon discover this place was also very dangerous as organized crime is very prevalent. The drug cartels were constantly gunning each other down to gain dominance, fighting to keep control of what they deemed their territory. U.S. citizens have been the victims of many violent crimes such as homicide, kidnapping, carjacking and robbery.

My brother found himself in a grave situation, lying face up on a dusty side street. Frank had his hands up as if surrendering. Three members of a known drug cartel were staring down at him while he froze staring up into the barrel of a pistol. He was in the wrong place at the wrong time. My brother knew he was going to be the next victim if he couldn't talk them out of killing him.

Frank glanced around as he saw the locals scurrying away with their heads down. He saw men running for cover and women whisking their children into buildings for safety. They were avoiding another grisly scene not wanting to get involved, afraid for their own lives and the lives of their families. Soon, the streets were empty and he saw no help on the horizon.

These three outlaws were complaining because they were still a little drunk and starting to feel the effects of a hangover from heavy drinking just a few hours before. They were talking among themselves that if they shot him they would have to dispose of Frank's body which was messy and time consuming. It was a hot, muggy morning.

They were all overweight, out of shape and just weren't in the mood for all that work. By the way they spoke, it was clear these men had killed many others in the past and they seemed to regard life as having little or no value.

As precious seconds were ticking by, Frank had to think fast! Soon, Uncle Art's voice echoed in Frank's memory that *someday the tiger claw could save your life!* He found his angle, hoping it would work. He took the opportunity as he tried to convince these three in Spanish he would give them something of great value if they let him go. He promised he would leave town immediately and guaranteed his captors their boss would never know if they killed him or not. The boss wanted Frank dead because he perceived my brother to be a threat to their illegal drug operation.

This piqued their interest as they agreed to Frank's offer if he had something they wanted in exchange for his life.

Frank slipped the tiger claw necklace off and gave it to the leader of the three men. While still holding the gun in his right hand, the leader took the necklace in his left hand. Frank watched as a broken tooth, yellow smile formed across the gunman's sweaty face as he examined it for a moment. He smiled big as he held it up to the sunlight admiring his new gift while his companions nodded and smiled too. Still holding the gun with his finger close to the trigger, this man carelessly used both hands as he slipped the necklace over his head and placed it around his neck.

Frank had hope as it appeared the gift was acceptable trade for his life. The gun was quickly tucked under the leader's belt on his right side just beyond his big, overlapping belly. The three thugs turned and walked away laughing, threatening they would kill him if they ever saw him again! Frank believed every word.

Within the hour he breathed a big sigh of relief as he sat safely belted in his seat, still wearing his dusty clothes. He closed his eyes as he felt the thrust of the plane pull him gently into his seat at takeoff. The familiar whine of the jet engines rang in his ears as he headed for home.

For no weapon formed against you shall prosper... (Isaiah 54:17)

I have offered up prayers for family and friends for protection and have asked God to reveal Himself to them through dreams, visions and other mean of His choosing. I declare the Holy Spirit will soften their hearts before, so they will be open to receiving Jesus as their Lord and Savior forever changing their eternity. I pray God will call them unto Him through a prayer of salvation to establish a strong relationship with the Lord. Praying in the mornings, I ask God to send ministers, angels, and others who have God's truth to speak to my loved ones, friends and even strangers. I ask God to send people who have His wisdom and who have the boldness and revelation to speak to my friends and family. I have seen many prayers answered and I am grateful.

My brother and I might have different perspectives for the moment about how the end result came about. Perhaps Frank believes he was clever and lucky to have talked his way out of this life threatening ordeal.

I see it differently. I believe God saved his life. My Uncle Art declared the tiger claw could save his life someday. That hints at the prophetic, but this is exactly what happened. I've been alerted so many times to pray for my brother's safety. Many times I have asked Frank what happened at a particular time when the Lord prompted me to pray.

I have heard many stories of near disaster as Frank has told me he somehow lived through many life-threatening circumstances. It was always God coming to Frank's aid.

The power of prayer is amazing! Many family members have come to the Lord and I'll see them in Heaven. We are to give thanks to God at all times and I am happy to have my brother in my life.

Nobody knows for sure what happens in the spiritual realm, but I believe Frank survived not from a lucky break or being smart. I believe it was the power of God's favor on my brother's life that he lived through this ordeal and is still here today. Scripture tells me to pray, believe and receive. Scripture also tells me to give thanks to God in all things and I do.

If you abide in Me and My words abide in you, ask whatever you wish and it will be done for you.
(John 15:7)

Ask Yourself...

- *Can I clearly see how God answers my prayers for protection much like the author can in this testimony?*
- *Do I truly believe God's word used as prayer will change my problems?*
- *Can I create a habit to use scriptures to pray protection over my family and friends?*
- *What are my favorite promise scriptures–the ones I use the most?*
- *Can I see the benefits of adding more scriptures to my arsenal?*

-34-

Mom in Heaven

My daughter, Alicia, pushed a chair closer, positioning herself close to Mom's ear while choosing her words with great care. Alicia gently laid her head on the bed close to Mom's ear. While she softly spoke of the joys, she quoted calming scriptures from the Bible of what Mom could expect in her near future.

Alicia created wonderful visions allowing Mom's thoughts to drift toward her new home. Mom lay there with her eyes closed, listening and dreaming of what she heard as she savored the vivid images created by Alicia's stories.

Each word was another brush stroke, each sentence a scene, all working together to bring glimpses of Mom's eternity in glorious Heaven. Mom was close to death and this was a beautiful goodbye to one of my best friends. Alicia's words soothed her unease and calmed her uncertainty by painting word pictures of Heaven. Mom was ready and it would be soon.

Alicia soothed Mom's tired body and mind through her constant, loving touch massaging her back, neck and mostly her head hour after hour in the last five days of Mom's life. Mom loved to be massaged as it gave her so much comfort.

Through Alicia's spoken word, Mom's thoughts raced ahead as she anticipated the thought of the grand homecoming she knew was waiting for her in Heaven. Mom envisioned being surrounded by so many loved ones who gave their lives to Jesus and passed on before her.

When I came to visit, I pushed a chair close to her hospital bed and laid my head as close to hers as I could and began massaging too.

Mom collected what little energy she could muster to ask for one thing.

In a strained, weak voice, she'd look my way and whisper, "Stories!"

She'd shut her eyes in exhaustion as speaking that one word robbed all her energy. Mom listened as I created lovely visions of our life together as they drew her back in time. She lay in her hospital bed reliving those cherished memories.

Mom had given her life to Jesus exactly three years earlier and she became a different person from that moment on. She was bedridden and had terrible eyesight. Her vision so weak that she couldn't read the large print Bible I bought her days after she gave her life to Jesus. Mom's hearing was so poor she couldn't hear me on the phone.

Until she repeated the prayer of salvation, she wanted nothing to do with God and said as much. I had very limited access to her in those last three years of her life. Even so, she seemed to catch up, spiritually speaking, as the Spirit of God was her teacher.

I sent her my written testimonies while I wrote this book and she was awestruck and kept asking why I hadn't shared these with her before. We'd both laugh as she forgot how she walked in darkness for the first eighty two years of her life. Mom had a total transformation and quickly became a seasoned believer with a deep knowledge of the spiritual things of God. Almost overnight she understood my prophetic and seer gifts as she realized she had these undeveloped God-given gifts too.

My mother died on her eighty-fifth birthday. A half hour after she passed away, my brother, Frank, met me at my house.

With huge, teary eyes Frank questioned, "I wonder where Mom is now?"

I said, "I don't wonder, I *know* where she is. She's in Heaven!"

He quietly asked, "But how do you know for sure?"

Frank listened to me as I reminded him of all the testimonies about us and how God had been declaring His presence to Frank his whole life. We talked for over an hour as I reminded him that there were many incidents in which he shouldn't have made it out alive as there was no logical possibility for his survival. Frank nodded his head in agreement as I explained that it was always God who saved him. Frank listened to every word I had to say as he fully comprehended and remembered each incident.

I also reminded him that while Mom was repeating the prayer of salvation, two people in the living room were pushing and screaming at each other. Frank knew these two people well and realized this incident was so out of character for them. Frank had to wonder if I was correct in my assumption that the devil had used them to create a diversion. Mom's passing was very serious to Frank and he wanted to talk about eternity and I took this chance to explain the truth. Mom's prayer of salvation changed her eternal destiny from Hell to Heaven.

"Frank," I said quietly, "I have been praying for you, Mom and everyone else in our family for over thirty years."

Frank nodded again and seemed to be satisfied Mom was, indeed, in Heaven. I believe God used that opportunity to plant seeds of faith in Frank through the word of my testimony.

As soon as Frank left for his hotel room to get some sleep, I laid down on the couch in exhaustion to nap for an hour. Thanking God that my mother was in Heaven, I quietly rested on the couch with my eyes closed. I was in shock a little as it is always a surprise when a loved one passes away even when it is inevitable. I knew I would start crying in grief any minute.

I shut my eyes and God gifted me a beautiful vision of Mom in Heaven. She appeared to be twenty-years-old again and her black hair shone like silk. She wore a broad smile on her youthful face. She was busy working, bent over slightly as she worked beside other saints in Heaven. She was talking, laughing and having a wonderful time. A blue or green sash was tied around her small waist, accenting a plain, white gown that reached the floor. The long, billowing sleeves of the pale robe widened gradually toward her wrists. Mom was young and beautiful again!

Mom became a citizen of Heaven that afternoon. There is no more suffering, no more tears or pain where I'll join her and many others much later.

Several weeks after Mom died, I talked to Alicia and confessed that I hadn't cried over Mom's passing and that these comforting visions of Mom had decreased over time and have since stopped. Alicia explained that God was healing my heart because I could see how happy she is in Heaven and I don't need these visions anymore. Alicia was right!

*He will transform the body of our humble
condition into the likeness of His glorious body...*
(Philippians 3:21 HCSB)

Ask Yourself...

- *Do I have the assurance that my loved ones will be in Heaven?*
- *Are there those in my family I need to speak boldly about God's love?*
- *Can I pray and ask the Lord what I need to do for my loved ones?*
- *Do I truly believe the Lord will give me the opportunity and the words to speak?*
- *Am I willing to take that bold step in faith not knowing the end results?*

-35-

Beautiful!

A few years ago, I was listening to our assistant pastor, Patti, speak. I loved her sermon that Sunday morning. Patti always spoke with such passion for the Lord.

She leaned in toward the congregation as she made eye contact with as many of us as she could.

With such conviction, she asked, "Do you want to know how God sees you? Ask Him! He'll tell you!"

As I lay in bed the next morning after my prayer time, I decided to ask God how He sees me. I shut my eyes and lifted my hands to receive all He had for me.

With reverence and total faith that I would hear my answer, I asked the Lord, "How do You see me?"

Immediately, He gave me this crystal clear vision. I saw myself as a twenty-year-old woman framed by a white background. My hairstyle matched my current style, falling to my shoulders in shining, light brown waves. I was wearing a long sleeved, black bodysuit. The suit was woven with symmetrical energy currents which glowed white, silver and gold which is the living power of the Spirit. These currents and the suit they were set into were spiritual skin, as much a part of me as my hands or feet.

At the same time, I heard the Lord say, "Beautiful!"

Beautiful, young and full of joy, I could tell I was adored by our Father in Heaven. I felt beautiful too! I will always have this snapshot of how special I am to God. When I need a shot of joy in my life to combat ill feelings I always go to this vision. I'm sure that was God's intent all along.

The following Sunday after church, our newly-formed, twelve-member, prophetic team had a meeting at my home. The leader had us all form two lines facing each other. We were to ask the Spirit for one word describing the person standing in front of us. We were to each share the word we received for that person then take a step to the right and do the same for the next person until we had spoken God's word over everyone and they had spoken over us.

Pastor Paul nervously smiled, diverted his eyes from me and quietly mumbled, "Beautiful," as he quickly side-stepped. toward the next person in line. I smiled at the confirmation!

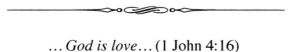

… God is love… (1 John 4:16)

Ask Yourself…

- *How do I see myself?*
- *Have I ever asked God how He sees me?*
- *Am I willing to do so and believe He will show me?*
- *Do I see this might have lasting value changing my self-perception?*

-36-

Counterfeit Gifts

I knew I had special gifts, but became influenced by the world. Soon forgetting where these gifts originated, I wanted answers. This has happened to many others. Not being fed the word of God, fellowshipping with other believers, attending church or praying will leave us open to any strange interpretation.

This is where the devil shows up and the power behind these godly gifts can be tainted and even used by the enemy. I wasn't aware of the enemy's tactics. This was a trap and I was walking toward that snare.

The Bible tells us not to practice fortunetelling, use sorcery, interpret omens, engage in witchcraft, cast spells or function as mediums or psychics. We are not to call for the spirits of the dead as these things are all detestable in the sight of the Lord.

Psychic or Seer?

At nineteen-years-old, I started to confuse my God-given gifts of being prophetic and a seer with being a psychic. Not fully understanding the difference, I wanted answers. Something deep inside told me going forward was wrong, but I didn't fully understand where this thought came from and decided to investigate.

Wanting to develop what I thought was my natural gift to see into the future, I thought I'd wait for a class somewhere to help explain things. Wouldn't you know it! An advertisement in the newspaper was offering a class in Portland on this subject and it caught my attention! I decided to go to the class for developing psychic abilities after work the next week.

Heading to the Class

It was a cold and rainy evening in the middle of winter. After an hour of searching, I found the rundown, two-story house with an old, beat-up sign in its front lawn. I was wearing high heels, a dress and a coat and looked completely out of place in this old, dangerous neighborhood.

As I slowly walked toward the house, I noticed flickering candles inside sitting on the unpainted, cracked window ledge to light the house. There were no cars in front, nor could I see or hear anyone inside. I walked up the creaking, unpainted, wooden stairs to the front door. This street and house reminded me of the beginning of a horror film. Taking one step after another my curiosity compelled me to go forward. I was also aware that my foolish actions could lead to something ghastly, but I couldn't comprehend what it might be as I continued.

My heart was beating fast and my eyes were wild with fright. I had an urge to run away from that place. However, I was still curious about what was waiting for me inside.

Taking a moment to make my final decision to enter or go home, I quickly glanced at the outside of the house from the covered porch. Old wind chimes were tinkling from the stormy weather, dandelions and grass grew along the cracked sidewalk and the window screens were rusty and torn. The door had a sign on it indicating I should walk in for the introductory class. I politely knocked anyway and then walked into this eerie, old house. I stood nervously in the foyer. I could hear a group of people in another room saying something in unison which disturbed my spirit.

The Bible explains that the devil offers counterfeit gifts. Some of these counterfeit gifts are tarot cards, Ouija boards, fortune telling, reading horoscopes, psychics, conjuring spells and calling upon the dead as a medium would do. These are from the enemy and are not from God. Witchcraft is the use of magical powers, especially obtained by evil spirits.

Also he made his son pass through the fire, practiced soothsaying, used witchcraft and consulted spiritists and mediums. He did much evil in the sight of the Lord, to provoke Him to anger.
(2 Kings 21:6)

Sin seems to muffle the voice of the Lord. The more steps we take toward that sin the harder our hearts become and the weaker the voice of God will become. We will soon have less guilt and the sin will eventually have a stronghold on us and could control us. Guard yourself and don't take that first step.

The Lord will deliver me from every evil work and preserve me for His Heavenly Kingdom. To Him be glory forever and ever! Amen!
(2 Timothy 4:18)

Having no peace about entering that house of witchcraft was my personal alarm from the Spirit trying to guide me away to safety. I was being lulled into believing the lies of the enemy. The devil's desire was to corrupt both me and my gifts. I had a strong sense I was heading down the wrong path. But I moved forward in my rebellion and this is sin.

Rebellion is as sinful as witchcraft. (1 Samuel 15:23)

Get Out of There, Now!

Having no peace didn't stop me, so the Spirit wasn't as gentle this time.

I heard the Spirit yell in an angry man's voice, "Get out of here, now!"

I heard that loud and clear and became a little panicked. I turned around as quickly as I could in my high heels and shuffled out the door down the slippery, wet stairs. Then I ran to my car and headed for home.

Living my life far away from God, I was vulnerable enough to become entangled into the enemy's web of lies and deceit. The Spirit was loud and clear that evening keeping me safe from whatever lured me inside that place of darkness. The Lord allowed me to drive to this terrible place before warning me, so I'd remember this incident with all the negative feelings.

The spirit of witchcraft will lead people away from God into darkness, hopelessness and despair. This is sin and Jesus said, "Whoever commits a sin is a slave of sin" (John 8:34). Jesus also said, "The enemy is here to kill, steal and destroy" (John 10:10). The devil uses sin to keep us trapped in shame, secrets and keeps us from lifting our head up to God. In Romans 8:6 it teaches us that when we follow what the world offers it brings death, but God gives us peace and life when we set our mind to follow His instructions.

I will put an end to all witchcraft, and there will be no more fortune-tellers. (Micah 5:12)

Ask Yourself...

- *Am I aware that a single step toward sin could lead to a long-term bad habit?*
- *Have I ever taken that first step toward rebellion in my past and where did it lead me?*
- *Am I aware that the enemy is here to offer me sin to kill, steal and destroy?*
- *Have I asked God to forgive me and asked for His help?*

-37-

Failed Scam

My husband and I have offered bedrooms in our home to international students who attended one of the English immersion programs in our area. I was contacted through my website and was sent a picture of a cute woman and her daughter who claimed the daughter received a full six-month scholarship at a local university. The email claimed the young woman wanted to stay at our house for the entire time and go to school. I agreed and the check for the whole amount was mailed to my home.

A week later, I received a bank check from the UK and deposited it even though a red flag popped up as there was no return address on the envelope. I rationalized it was from a different country with different ideas.

A few days after the five thousand dollar check cleared, I saw signs that it might be a scam. Using a flimsy excuse, they were asking me to return the whole amount through a wire transfer stating they didn't want the young woman at our home anymore. *Hmmm!*

A thought zipped through my mind from the Spirit. He gave me a very specific warning that I should not wire transfer any money to these people. I didn't understand, so I kept the cash at home and decided to pray and investigate this situation.

For the Lord your God is going with you! He will fight for you against your enemies, and He will give you victory!
(Deuteronomy 20:4)

Brilliant, Witty and Fun Answer from God!

I prayed about this matter and also prayed regarding my writing of the evil power behind psychics in the previous chapter called *Counterfeit Gifts*.

At the tail end of that prayer, I heard the Spirit ask me, "What's the difference between a psychic and a seer?" (I am a seer as I see visions from God and into the spiritual realm)

I smiled as it sounded a little bit like a joke. I responded out loud, "I don't know. What?"

The Spirit replied, "One reads palms and the other reads Psalms!" (Psalms is a book in the Bible)

God knew I'd love his quick-witted question and answer as I laughed out loud with delight. I continued writing. Ten minutes later, it hit me. All of a sudden, I tilted my head to the right and looked to the left as another idea came to me. Was God asking me to find a scripture in the book of Psalms?

I grabbed my Bible laying on the desk and opened it. I noticed it flipped open to Psalms. I never do this and wouldn't advise it for accurate results, but I shut my eyes and simply asked God to show me what He wanted me to read. God led me to the following scripture which appeared to be highlighted in bold and fit perfectly for my troubles.

As I began to read, I realized it was a plea from David to God for protection. I took this scripture and prayed it several times a day as I knew this prayer was my protection against the scammers too.

Deliver me, O Lord, from evil men;
Preserve me from violent men,
Who plan evil things in their hearts;
They continually gather together for war.
They sharpen their tongues like a serpent;
The poison of asps is under their lips.

Keep me, O Lord, from the hands of the wicked;
Preserve me from violent men,
Who have purposed to make my steps stumble.
The proud have hidden a snare for me, and cords;
They have spread a net by the wayside;
They have set traps for me.
(Psalms 140:1-5)

Isn't it amazing how God can weave two separate issues into one clever response giving me a prayer to cover my troubles? I knew God had this situation covered, but I still had to do my part until this problem was resolved. I taped this prayer on the wall just above my computer and prayed it over my family and friends.

I recognized that my situation fell under the category of spiritual warfare. My path became very clear as I knew I was just one of many they were scamming at the same time. I prayed this prayer covering us all asking for protection in the physical, financial and emotional arenas.

How My Scam Ended

Refusing to wire their money, this group harassed and threatened my family and me for over a week. Knowing they were only after money, I had to rely heavily on the Lord and keep repeating the scripture He sent me. God was my refuge, but it was still a frightening time for me. I suffered in silence as I was embarrassed to be in this situation.

My bank kept advising me to wire the money back, but I knew better. I finally spoke to the fraud department.

They told me this transaction was probably a scam and if I wired the money back, the scammers would happily contact their bank in England, sign a Hold Harmless document and state that I was the fraud. This document is a demand that the full amount be returned to whoever issued the check.

Under bank rules and regulations my bank would comply and return another five thousand dollars. My bank would chase me for that amount and I would be deemed a fraud and could face stiff penalties under the law.

Neither bank would care that I already wired the money back as that would be deemed a separate transaction. The scammers would have made a quick five grand in under a week.

I sent the bad guys a simple email with two words on it – Hold Harmless. Knowing I was on to them they signed the document and received their money back from my bank. I reimbursed my bank the same day and the whole storm blew over and the bad guys didn't steal a penny from me. Whew, I'm grateful to God to have escaped that evil scam!

My advice is to be careful and don't take foreign or local checks from people you don't know. New scams are carefully being crafted all the time.

Give all your troubles to God and He will deliver you from evil men, bloodthirsty men who have sinister schemes planned with bribes in their right hands. I have stepped up my prayers and pray more protection over my family and friends now.

Though I am surrounded by troubles, you will protect me from the anger of my enemies. You reach out your hand, and the power of your right hand saves me.
(Psalms 138:7)

Ask Yourself…

- *Do I have the faith that I can simply give my troubles to God through daily prayer, declarations and cover it with scripture?*
- *Am I aware that after I pray and receive an answer from God I still need to diligently do my part?*
- *Have I taken the time to search scripture and pray these as promises over myself and others?*

-38-

Glenn and Karen

I n the early 1970s it was easy to fall in love and even easier in high school. Glenn and Karen shared an uncommon love as they lived a little differently than me. I didn't understand them, but became curious as they seemed to have a different calling, a higher calling than me.

At a mere glance it was easy to see Glenn and Karen walked in the true love they held for each other. They were stronger together than apart. God seemed to knit these two souls together as one as they walked through life and put their trust in God alone. These two were planning on marrying after they graduated high school.

Let your light so shine before men, that they may see your good works and glorify your Father in Heaven.
(Matthew 5:16)

They were holding hands as the three of us walked along that dirt path through a beautiful park on the way to her house. It was only about a mile from my house to Karen's house. We were in the middle of a small stand of trees in the park where several runoff creeks trickled after a few days of hard rain. We all took care as we stepped across these little creeks laughing as we all got our feet a little damp. I noticed Glenn slowed the pace down and I wondered why.

He made a few comments about how people were calling him a Jesus freak. Karen nodded in agreement and glanced at Glenn with that special couple-in-love look of acknowledgement. I could see she and Glenn had communicated. Still not understanding, I silently listened. Karen was quiet as well, occasionally glancing at her beloved, obviously proud of him as he began to talk to us about Jesus. She only dared to take a few quick glances in my direction to see my reaction to what Glenn was saying. She could tell I was interested as I had never seen this side of them before.

Glenn stared straight ahead and started mumbling to himself out loud about how he might be a Jesus freak. I could tell he was using me to practice what they taught him at church. He was pretending he was figuring this all out at that moment.

I knew he was preaching to me as he said, "After all, I am following Jesus. He is my Lord and Savior. He died on the cross to pay for all my sins and saved me from death and Hell." He announced to us as his voice was full of conviction, "Well, I guess I am a Jesus freak!"

Glenn turned toward me and asked, "So what's wrong with being a Jesus freak?"

I quietly shrugged my shoulders as I had never thought about it before. I wanted to think about all I heard from Glenn that afternoon as this ten minutes was unforgettable.

Seeing the passion in Glenn and Karen, I knew they were on to something great. They acted like the most natural and exciting subject for them to talk about was their love of Jesus. They were walking the road of faith together.

Glenn mentioned, "After all, striving to be the best version of myself for Jesus could only be considered great and would surely make our future better, right?"

I nodded. Something big inside of me was stirring as I remembered how I'd had those same feelings so many years earlier. My faith sat dormant and withered ever since our family moved out west and we stopped attending church years earlier.

Glenn was so open and vulnerable as he shared his whole heart even though he knew I could scoff at him. Most of us at that age were snide and sarcastic to each other. I had to admire Glenn as he had no idea how I'd react to his statements, but he stepped up anyway and planted a seed of faith in me.

In my early twenties, I talked with a Christian woman. She didn't try to hide the fact that she didn't care for me. The conversation turned to God. Being untrained and unchurched, I wanted to spew what I now know was my garbage theology. Telling her that I *knew* the God of Bible wasn't real and I had my own thoughts and shared a few with her.

She listened quietly and respectfully and her only response was, "But what if you're wrong!"

I knew she was alerting me that my eternal life was in jeopardy. After five times of hearing the same rebuttal, we both stopped talking. Her message wasn't delivered in a loving way, but I never forgot her words. God inserted them into my heart and added them to the pile of other truths the Lord stored in my heart. He resurrected those truths years later when I gave my life to Jesus again through a prayer of salvation.

Our lives are made up of many moments. Most of them are lived and then forgotten. Some moments are pointed out by God to be etched in our memories forever to bring about an important point. When more of these moments are added, it brings about a pattern. This story was one of those fleeting but important recollections of a pattern God established in my life...people ministering to me about Jesus!

This seemingly insignificant time was carefully crafted and set up by God to plant seeds of faith in me. Hearing Glenn speak of Jesus touched my heart as I knew of his godly lifestyle and attendance at church. He spoke with such passion and love for Jesus, not sure if I would scoff at him which also made a big impression on me as a teenager. God meets us in the now, in every moment. Don't waste time, but instead redeem it and be ready for every moment to be surrendered to and used by the Lord.

Over the years, the Lord directed others in my path to add more seeds of faith. The Lord put people in front of me who knew Jesus and had the boldness to talk to me. It was interesting how, even though I was unaware of it, other believers could sense the Spirit living inside me ever since I gave my life to Jesus as a small child.

Now, there are those times when I plant seeds of faith to be nurtured and cared for by others down the road. Sometimes I don't see immediate results. I hope you realize that it is never a waste of time to share Jesus with others and they may always remember your efforts. If they don't remember, God surely will.

For He said to them, "Go into all the world and preach the gospel to every creature." (Mark 16:15)

Ask Yourself...

- *Can I remember a time in my life when someone stepped out of their comfort and spoke to me of their faith in Jesus?*
- *What is the one thing they said or did that makes me remember them?*
- *How can I have the same profound effect on someone when sharing Jesus with others?*
- *Am I willing to step out of my comfort zone in faith to share Jesus with others?*

-39-

Meeting Bernie

I used to laugh and tell my friends, "If God wants me to get married again, He'll have to hit me over the head with a two-by-four and point directly to the man!"

Then I'd laugh even more because I didn't think God was in the match making business. I thought God had more important things to do than help me find a man. I did preach to all my single friends to pray for their future spouses, but didn't think much further about that idea.

Years before, one of my good friends at our little church told me, "I'd only marry my best friend."

Wow, the Lord emphasized this idea and I made it my own.

Another friend, James, was prophetic and part of our group of friends. He heard from the Lord often. He emailed me one day and as he was typing, he said the Spirit took over and had a message for me.

"Great things are coming your way! The best is yet to come!"

Over the previous six months I heard this exact message from five other people. I paid attention and believed something great was around the corner for me.

I met Bernie a few months later at our Sunday afternoon Christian singles dance lessons. After our group of about twenty learned country and western dances we all started frequenting a local cowboy dance club. Bernie and I became dance partners and once a week had so much fun with our friends while we danced the night away.

Bernie and I started to meet early and share dinner before the dance started. Our relationship bloomed over those weekly platters of nachos.

We seemed to have so much in common. We were even a great match in spiritual aspects. Bernie and I had been faced with the same difficult situations in our past. We shared similar experiences and even outcomes.

Someone abused his loved one and Bernie couldn't shake the desire that he wanted to hurt that man.

It took many weeks, but with the help of his brothers in Christ at his men's Bible study, Bernie had a breakthrough. He was healed one night and all his anger melted away. He gave his life to the Lord and became more intimate with God.

This ultimately built Bernie's faith and after this experience, he was baptized. I had a similar experience and God used it to teach me and build my faith too.

After a few months of dating, Bernie showed up for our date with a vase of flowers and two cards. Bernie said, "I didn't know which one to get, so I bought them both!"

On one of the cards he wrote, *"The Best Is To Come! The Best from Me, Bernie."* On the other card he wrote, *"Going to be your best friend, Bernie."* I liked them both and put them next my coat as we danced the night away.

It wasn't until the next morning that I started thinking about what Bernie wrote.

"Hey, wait a minute," I said out loud, so full of excitement.

I hurried to gather the cards and compared them with the printed prophetic email James sent me months before that I kept in my Bible. I realized they matched perfectly. Only God knew I had these two sentiments in my heart. I had never verbalized them to anyone and I certainly didn't put them together until this moment.

It couldn't be coincidence that both of those prophetic words could come from Bernie. No, this was my "two-by-four moment." I asked God if He wanted me to marry again to make it clear and point to the man He wanted me to marry. So many other things seemed to line up and it seemed undeniably like this was the man for me. I eventually showed the email from James to Bernie and told him what I thought. Bernie was happy to have this confirmation too. We were excited to start our new lives together.

Our Very First Conversation

Bernie has been a General Contractor for over forty years. Bernie started telling me a story, "Years ago my cousin and I were contracted to work at the ski lodge at…"

I immediately remembered something fairly odd, but important to us both as I interrupted him, "Bernie, I'm sorry to interrupt, but was this back in February of 1973 or so?"

Bernie thought a second and said, "Yes, how did you know?"

"Can I tell you my story first? I think it's an important memory."

He nodded his head yes and I could see he was intrigued.

I told Bernie that I was an avid skier and in 1973 I was at Timberline Lodge most weekends in the winter. Sometimes I'd go night skiing after work on Fridays, which might be the time of my odd and somewhat important story. In my late teens, I came in to take a break from skiing. I opened a locker and found a cheap, abandoned camera.

Two men on scaffolding were working on the walls and ceilings a few feet away from this locker.

I peered up and asked those two men, "I found this camera. Is it yours?"

"Nope," they said still working.

"*Hmm!*" I thought and then asked, "Are you sure?"

Still working they responded, "Not ours!"

This was Bernie and his cousin. I've always thought it was strange that I would remember a ten-second encounter with two men that I really didn't even see. It's amusing to think that God arranged this unforgettable and brief encounter with my future husband over twenty years before we met.

"For My thoughts are not your thoughts, nor are your ways My ways," says the Lord. (Isaiah 55:8)

God inserted this moment in my memory, so I would remember it at the right time. It appears to have been another "two-by-four encounter." This seemingly unimportant interaction is so vivid in my mind that I can recall most of the details of the scene today.

Then the Lord God said, "It is not good for the man to be alone. I will make a helper who is just right for him."
(Genesis 2:18)

Ask Yourself...

- *Have I had my own "two-by-four" moments with God?*
- *How has it impacted my life and faith in God?*
- *Have I shared my two-by-four testimony with others as an opening to share Jesus with them?*
- *What are the long-term results of sharing my faith with others?*
- *Is there anything stopping me from doing so?*

Section Six:

Frightening Encounters–Saving Women

...that we may be delivered from evil and wicked men.
(2 Thessalonians 3:2)

A worthless person, a wicked man,
Walks with a perverse mouth;
He winks with his eyes,
He shuffles his feet,
He points with his fingers;
Perversity is in his heart,
He devises evil continually,
He sows discord.
Therefore his calamity shall come suddenly;
Suddenly he shall be broken without remedy.
(Proverbs 6:12-15)

God used me to stop evil men from abusing, torturing, kidnapping and killing women. At least three men appeared to be serial murderers, possibly more. There were nine incidents involving ten men. God chose to place me at the scene seconds before the perpetrators started. I have chosen three testimonies to share.

These testimonies are frightening. Not wanting to promote violence, I am keeping most of the details to myself as my purpose is not to glorify my martial arts skills, but to glorify God. The Lord sees it all and those evildoers were given what they gave other women which was unbridled brutality. They received harsh penalties here on earth and were stopped by God through me, a woman. I've heard from other men that those evil men who were beaten by me lost all confidence in their abilities and surely stopped their evil towards women.

I pray that through their physical and emotional brokenness they repented and submitted to the call through the blood of Jesus accepting eternal salvation. I believe this was the end result for most of these abusers of women.

Do not fear those who kill the body but are unable to kill the soul; but rather fear Him who is able to destroy both soul and body in hell. (Matthew 10:28)

-40-

Almost Kidnapped

Going to the gym and martial arts class three afternoons every week was exhausting! I loved exercising and martial arts and this was my routine for two and a half years. I was in great shape and I could fight. I didn't care to take the tests to get the higher belts.

Being in the best shape of my life, I was confident that I would be able to handle myself if any problems came up. Little did I know that my confidence would someday be put to the test.

In the Bible it speaks of Philip baptizing the Ethiopian eunuch, "*...they went down into the water and Philip baptized him. When they came up out of the water, the Spirit of the Lord snatched Philip away...*" (Acts 8:38-39). This Ethiopian realized that Philip was needed elsewhere and knew God physically transported him to another place. The Ethiopian understood exactly what happened the moment it occurred and he was filled with joy.

Very Strange Encounter

I had a similar experience much like Philip as I was transported to another place where I was needed. One moment I was at home getting ready to make dinner in my kitchen. In a blink of an eye, I found myself completely confused, but standing on a street many miles from home in another city. I had a moment to glance around and saw my parked car across the street.

Stunned, I searched my mind trying to make sense of what just happened. Several seconds later, my attention was diverted as a woman's shrieks for help reached my ears. My confusion turned to understanding and I was ready to help. I whirled around to detect where the woman was as I spotted this terrifying scene down the street from me.

She screamed with all her might as I heard, "HELP ME! HELP ME! HEEEEELP!" This was happening right before my eyes and I was shocked. I witnessed this dreadful scene of a man dragging her from left to right, from the sidewalk to his waiting vehicle.

The kidnapper appeared scruffy as he dressed in dirty, old jeans and a plaid work shirt. He used a baseball cap to hide his face. Both the driver's door and the big, roll-down door were open. He was all prepped and set for a quick and easy kidnapping of his next intended victim.

He was dragging her by the back of her coat collar, face up like a sack of garbage as she helplessly screamed and kicked in terror with no one around to help except me. He appeared relaxed as though he had done this many times before. Not acting like he was in a hurry, he didn't keep watch for other people. Nobody had stopped him before and it probably took him under a minute to kidnap any woman he fancied.

The Spirit told me that this wasn't his first time. I believe he was a serial killer of women. It appeared he used the same system right down to the last detail for a quick kidnapping and an easy escape.

It became my job to save her from certain doom. I ran the quarter block to her as hard and fast as I could. I was filled with holy and righteous anger at what he had planned for this innocent woman. I sensed nobody would have ever known what happened to her like many other women before. It was frightening, but I was prepared.

When I reached him, I knocked him down, kicked and punched him as hard as I could with all my strength. I struck his face, legs, ribs and arms breaking bones, so he couldn't get up. I was his monster in the dark and I was more than happy to help this distressed woman.

...when the wicked are cut off, you shall see it.
(Psalms 37:34)

In the background, I heard her faintly thanking me for helping her. All my attention was still on the kidnapper.

After several minutes of pummeling him, I suddenly felt compelled to stop. Not understanding why I stopped, I still wanted to end his life and his reign of terror on his future victims, but I was done. I stood over him as I breathed hard, damp with sweat, peering down at him as the winner. My hands were still curled into fists.

I saw the woman out of the corner of my eye as she stood up, found her shoe, slipped it back on and almost fell over because of the attack. She swayed clumsily just barely able to limp over to me. She stood almost shoulder to shoulder to my left. While moaning and whimpering, her body was shaking with tremors. I noticed scrapes and blood on her legs from being drug on the sidewalk and street.

She and I peered down at this monster lying helplessly on the street. She stared at him for a long time and breathed heavily as if trying to make sense of the attack. I turned my head and looked at her.

Her clothes were ripped and wet, covered with street grime, a mix of oil, filth and rain water. Her hair, makeup and clothes had become tattered and I noticed her nylons were shredded and hanging off her legs. She was confused and in shock by the attack.

I was angry at this man as I turned to glare down at him again. I was grateful to be in the middle of this attack to stop him from kidnapping her and from harming anymore women.

We both turned our attention from this predator to glance at his van, still parked on the street. The hair stood up on the back of my neck. I didn't want to see inside this chamber of horrors knowing I would never get that image out of my mind.

With stoic looks, the woman and I glanced at each other for several seconds. Moments before, she had been dressed in fine clothes and heels, wearing a dress with an expensive jacket all buttoned up. Her hair and makeup were probably stunning and she was dressed as if she were on her way to one of the fine restaurants of the area. I could see this nicely dressed, young woman was in her twenties.

Still out of breath and trying to regain my composure, I gave him a five-second glare. He was down for the count and unable to get up! I thought to myself, *Job well done!*

She asked me several times, "What do you think he wanted?"

Knowing she was still in shock, I didn't respond as I waited for her mind to catch up to her current situation. I didn't answer. When she asked me for a third time what the man wanted, the predator started groaning on the side of the street next to his van.

I paused to allow her to collect her thoughts before saying, "I think you know what he wanted."

Too little time had passed and she didn't comprehend the situation yet. She thought about what I said for a few seconds and then gasped as she finally understood.

Bent on revenge, this woman knelt down and beat him furiously. I don't know what happened after that other than she was fine, he was injured and unable move.

He let out a few groans as I turned and ran as hard and fast as I could to my vehicle. I only slowed down enough to check over my shoulder to make sure I wasn't being chased.

When justice is done, it is a joy to the righteous, but terror to evildoers. (Proverbs 21:15 KJV)

Frightening Vision of the Predator

The Spirit showed me, in a vision that resembled a two-minute movie, that this man had kidnapped many other women. My vantage point was from about twenty feet away to his left as he faced right. He watched the street searching for his next victim through his side passenger window as he scanned the sidewalk. Driving slowly in the dark and rain, he was trolling for his next victim. He had no compassion and saw women as disposable.

He searched for a woman with a buttoned up jacket which created the perfect package. He could easily sneak up behind and grab her to take her down to the ground to drag her to his waiting vehicle. He was searching for a long haired woman and someone he thought wouldn't put up a fight in her nicer clothes.

He chose his van carefully. It was a dirty, old cube van which looked like a delivery truck with few windows. The Spirit also showed me that he chose that van which wouldn't be noticed. His whole kidnapping process could take as little as thirty seconds. This vision was a chilling scene.

Beloved, never avenge yourselves, but leave it to the wrath of God, for it is written, "Vengeance is mine, I will repay, says the Lord".
(Romans 12:19)

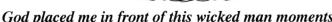

God placed me in front of this wicked man moments before he grabbed his next intended victim. The scene turned grisly and frightening as he was kidnapping her. Did this woman call out to Jesus for help? I have more questions than answers. All I understand is that I fulfilled my part in stopping this evildoer. Beyond these details, I have no other answers... only God knows the truth!

The wicked lie in wait for the righteous, intent on putting them to death. (Psalms 37:32)

Ask Yourself...

- *Life is difficult at times, but what can I thank God for today?*
- *Can I see the Lord used the author's troubled childhood from earlier stories to lead her to Karate lessons as an adult?*
- *How have I compensated because of past hurts?*
- *Can I see how this lines up with God creating her to be strong and brave?*
- *What skills has God given me for His purposes?*

Another Strange Encounter

It was eight o'clock at night and getting dark. I was at home that Friday night taking care of things around the house when the Lord chose to transport me to a local sporting event several towns over.

In a blink of an eye, I found myself standing outside the main attraction a hundred feet from the exit gate in the dimly lit parking area. I instantly recognized I had been transported as this was the second time it happened. I stood and wondered why I was placed in this dirt and grass parking lot after dark, but I calmly watched and waited. I had the distinct impression as to where my car was parked. I didn't turn around to verify as I just knew.

A tall, beautiful, blonde woman and a tall, handsome man came out from the main gate slowly meandering deeper into the dark parking lot. She was nearly six feet tall with a thin, red sweater and tight jeans. She was beautiful. He was a few inches taller and had a black, flannel shirt tucked into his tight jeans and wore cowboy boots and a hat. It appeared they both spent a fair amount of time at the gym as they both appeared trim and fit. They seemed to like each other as they were laughing and snuggling as they walked.

It was just the three of us and they walked slowly, giggling and snuggling as they made their way toward me through the dark. It appeared they were two people in love and soon they were about twenty feet in front of me. They still didn't seem to notice me as they strolled even closer.

Without warning, he flew into a rage as this man started beating her viciously with his fists like he wanted her dead. I assumed he wanted to lead her deeper into the darkness before he executed his plan. Either that or he became furious for some other reason during their short stroll.

My heart was racing at this shocking scene as I ran the twenty feet toward them. I stopped just short of them as she had fallen to the ground screaming in panic and pain while holding her hands up to protect her face. He was hunched down and using his fists to beat her with such fury. It appeared he wouldn't stop until she was dead.

Up close, I could see he had muscles with a lean frame. His adrenaline had kicked in quite strongly by that time. This was frightening to me as I wasn't sure I could take on such a brute and win.

I put my fighting skills to work and with all my power my first strike was to the outside and slightly behind his left knee as I struck him hard with my foot. Down he went as he yelled in pain. He stumbled and fell while I kicked and punched with all my might knowing that if I stopped it might give him an opening to retaliate. I kept at it until the job was done. He was injured and moaning with each punch or kick while using his arms to cover his face. I was trying to break bones to disable him, hoping to send him to the hospital.

"There is no peace," says the Lord, "for the wicked." (Isaiah 48:22)

As I was kicking and punching him, this woman was saying, "Thank you for helping me. I don't know why he wanted to hurt me. Who is he and why did he hit me?"

I realized as she spoke they didn't know each other. Within a few minutes, this evil man lay on the ground writhing in agony. Again, I wanted to keep hitting him, but for some strange reason I stopped.

Laying on the ground facing left, his broken left arm lay limp across his chest. I stood solid mostly unscathed. Curious to see who brutally beat him to the ground he pulled his right arm slightly down as he dared take a peek from the crook of his elbow which protected his eyes and face.

He peered up. I glared down at him with disgust with steely eyes, breathing heavily, my fists ready for another round. Horrified, he realized I was another woman. His ego was deflated which became a game changer for his evil sport of abusing women.

But the wicked are doomed, for they will get exactly what they deserve. (Isaiah 3:11)

I talked to the woman for half a minute. She told me she couldn't get up quite yet. Hearing a crowd of men yelling, I turned my attention toward the exit gate where a large group of men and women were running over to us to help. I didn't want to be involved. I jogged to my car and drove home only glancing back briefly to make sure I wasn't being followed.

Each time I stopped a man from abusing a woman, I felt compelled to run away and go home.

For evildoers shall be cut off; but those who wait on the Lord, they shall inherit the earth. (Psalms 37:9)

Ask Yourself...

- *Understanding the details in this story were unusual, am I confident enough in my relationship with God to do what He has called me to do no matter how extreme?*
- *Can I look back on circumstances knowing God prompted me to take action where I wouldn't have done so on my own?*
- *What were the results?*
- *Do I now have more confidence to take action when prompted by the Spirit?*

-42-

I Was Attacked!

My minivan ran out of gas when I was driving home from a dinner party. It stopped in a questionable and unfamiliar neighborhood next to a few bars. It was my fault as I thought I was too busy to stop for gas and was confident I could make it home on the fumes. It was after dark and I was far from home. I made a call and a tow truck with gas for my car was dispatched and would arrive shortly.

Not even a minute into my wait, a tall man about my age came out of thin air, grabbed my wrists and held them behind me. He marched me back behind an old building. I was partly in shock and partly wondering if this was a joke. A shorter man waited behind the building. I was puzzled as it appeared to be a setup, but there wasn't time for the two men to position themselves.

The shorter man walked slowly toward me from the dark shadows in the alley. His slow pace gave me time to formulate a plan of action. I remember thinking that I couldn't pick him out in a line-up if I had to because his face was twisted into a mask of utter hatred. I remember saying to myself, *What? He hates me? He doesn't even know me!*

My mind was paralyzed with fear and it was difficult to think. Within thirty seconds I had my confidence back realizing this was a real attack. *Really! They picked me? Well, aren't they in for a big surprise!* My training clicked in and I could think again.

The shorter man continued to walk toward me. He hunched over with his arms bent at the elbow and half stretched out ready to attack me. His fingers were bent claw-like and by the look on his face it appeared he wanted to tear me apart.

To do evil is like sport to a fool. (Proverbs 10:23)

With an evil laugh, he described in great detail how they were going to hurt me in a few different ways and put my life to an end. They let me know they had done these things to many other women. I had a strong sense that inciting all the fear they could muster up in their victims was part of their fun. I knew they had done atrocious things to many other women before they encountered me.

I kept my eyes focused on the shorter man's chest as I listened to him without a word or a response. I was in shock at what was happening, but mostly I was calculating the distance between us with each step he took. I had a great plan all cooked up in my mind with all the extra time they gave me. The favor of God keeps my enemies from defeating me as it speaks of in Psalms 41:11.

Before finishing his lengthy explanation, he walked into the perfect striking distance from me. I kicked him in the groin as hard as I could with my right foot.

"UH!" he moaned and toppled over into the filth on the ground, holding himself and writhing with pain.

Using the momentum from that kick, I raked my right heel down into the right shin of the man holding my arms behind me. He shouted in pain and let go of my wrists. I was so surprised how quick and easy it was to get away.

Behold, I have given you authority to tread on serpents and scorpions, and over all the power of the enemy, and nothing shall hurt you. (Luke 10:19)

When the taller man let go of my arms, he began to bend down to rub his leg. I thought to myself, *Wow, what a perfect opportunity!* I brought my right elbow up into his chin with all my strength.

I turned around and took a stride back and kicked him hard in the groin too. Down he went in the dirt and filth as he moaned and thrashed violently in pain.

> *The black night is their morning. They ally themselves*
> *with the terrors of darkness.* (Job 24:17)

I towered over them as I glared down at these two helpless perpetrators of evil. What was once their exciting sport had turned into their night of terror and one they wouldn't soon forget! As I stared down at them I wondered, *Now what do I do with them?* I knew I had to keep them down or I would have another fight on my hands. I stood thinking for another short moment. I was in control, something they surely understood by then.

They were on the filthy ground. This space appeared to be have been used by people who were up to no good for many years as I could see it was littered with liquor bottles, needles, and other debris.

These two loathsome abusers had both their hands covering themselves, fingers laced symmetrically for protection from me. It didn't help. I saw this as another invitation to make sure they were down, so I kicked the tall one as hard as I could again. I heard the bones in his fingers break. I was surprised at how bizarre and great it was to hear and feel his fingers break as he moaned in pain. I couldn't resist, so I struck him with all my might with my foot again.

What these monsters had done to other women was pure evil. The way the tall one had grabbed me and then marched me behind the building where the other one waited made me realize they had more experience than I wanted to think about. What they told me they had planned for me was unthinkable.

My heart was empty of any compassion or mercy for these torturers of women. Unbridled corruption fueled their actions and I was only too happy to end their reign of terror on other unsuspecting women. I took this chance to stop them with every bone I felt and heard break. I did this for all the victims of abuse.

I pulled the taller man by the bottom of the pant legs to line them up side by side. For some odd reason, I positioned them both facing the left. I carefully stepped over the tall man to get two more kicks in on the shorter man. That was three of my hardest kicks to the groin for each of them. I continued for another five minutes severely injuring one and then the other.

> *Do not be deceived, God will not be mocked; for whatever a man sows, that he will also reap.* (Galatians 6:7)

With horror, they were still watching, but unable to move anything other than their eyes and unable to moan too much as their broken ribs wouldn't allow them a big breath.

I couldn't explain why, but with precision left-foot balance on the uneven ground, I rested my right foot lightly across the neck of the taller man while staring deep into his eyes. As I stared at the tall man's neck, I was sure he could tell what I was thinking. His eyes were fixed on mine knowing what my next move would be. I was pondering whether I should end their pitiful, abusive lives or let them live.

My decision was made as I decided to crush his neck. All I had to do was lean in a little with my foot and watch the life drain from him while the shorter man watched in terror as he knew he would be next.

As soon as I made this decision, I stopped without any reason. I wanted to finish him off, but something held me back. Disappointed, I lifted my right foot off his neck. I was done.

Leaning over them with my sweetest smile, I said in a phony, patronizingly cheery voice, "Hey, boys, I have something for you in my car. Wait here, okay?"

Walking away, I smiled and laughed on the outside. On the inside, I was still trembling with fear at this terrifying incident. I imagined they were pretty frightened of what was to come next. I knew they were waiting and wondering if I was coming back with a tire iron or something sinister to finish them off. I was glad to end my encounter with these monsters.

Standing on the street, I rested my back against the corner of a nearby building close to my car. I could see and hear what was happening on all sides of me. I waited for what seemed like an hour for the tow truck. I heard no sounds from the men who still lay there unable to move. The minutes ticked by as I felt vulnerable and upset even though I was victorious over these two thugs. What I did to those two men wasn't natural for me.

When the tow truck finally arrived, we put gas in the minivan. I hopped in the front seat so quickly that I almost closed the door on my foot as I couldn't wait to get out of there. I was shaken, but relaxed a little more with every second away from the scene. I drove away into the night hoping I was done with those terrible men forever.

As I was fighting for my life and the lives of their future victims, it appeared to be too easy to get away from them. I wondered for years if I received help from the Lord, but assumed I'd never find the answer to that question.

Many sorrows shall be to the wicked, but he who trusts in the Lord, mercy shall surround him. (Psalms 32:10)

Ask Yourself...

- *Have I ever felt righteous anger because of the evil I witnessed?*
- *What did I do?*
- *What were the end results?*
- *What would I do next time?*
- *Have I allowed the Spirit to lead me in how to use this righteous anger productively?*

-43-

God's Secret Revealed

I tucked myself in bed that night and my last thought was marveling at why I was so untroubled about that evening's incident. I was grateful to have won the battle and glad it was over. As I lay there thinking about the attack, I started to drift off to sleep as the gentle rain tapped lightly against the windows. My old windows vibrated with an occasional gust of wind due to their old age.

It was out of character for me as I wasn't bothered in the least as I thought of those two men. These vicious men finally had the beating they deserved. I was content thinking of the two evil men who were surely still out there unable to get up and out of this rainstorm as I drifted off into peaceful slumber.

Give them the punishment they so richly deserve! Measure it out in proportion to their wickedness. Pay them back for all their evil deeds! Give them a taste of what they have done to others.
(Psalm 28:4)

Word of Explanation

Several years ago, I was being prayed over and ministered to by three women of my church. Toward the end of the counseling session, Linda, an acquaintance of mine from our church had a word for me from our Lord. It was a long and lengthy word, but this is the important part that referred to helping all those women -

I had a great life in my early childhood which quickly changed and my life became difficult. This was a long, rough time and I soon became a tough fighter. What I needed was for someone to fight for me, but I had to fight for others and myself. Those years were dark, but God was there with me every step of the way even though I was sometimes unaware or ignored Him.

I learned martial arts and I believed He created me to be strong and brave. God appointed me for the task of stopping all ten men as they began to perpetrate violence upon their chosen victims. He placed me in the mix of the violence to save many women from certain doom.

God also stopped me at the moment of His choosing so I would not kill these men. The Lord's plan was to bring them to a place of brokenness physically and emotionally. The beating they took from me brought them to a place of repentance opening their hearts to hear the good news of Jesus Christ. I believe this was God's plan all along. It was all God and very little of me. Over the years, I am understanding this more and more.

Wow, what a huge revelation from God! Until Linda's prophetic word, I didn't know for certain if it was God who orchestrated those encounters. This was my first confirmation. Her word was so specific and accurate.

Up until that afternoon, I had prayed many times as I had so many questions. Did I stop them permanently? Should I have killed them to save their future victims from such agony and death?

Through Linda's word from the Lord, all my questions were answered. God put me in front of all those evil men. He was the driving force behind me to break their bones. It was also God who stopped me at the exact moment in each case as His mission for me was fulfilled. God stopped me against my will in each case as I was ready to finish the job to end their abusive lives.

Another Word of Confirmation

Several years after this word from Linda, I visited a church close to our house with my friend, Valerie, to attend a Friday night service.

I'd never met Dean before that night. He is a prophetic man and he nodded pleasantly as he walked past me. Then he stopped, turned around and said he had a word from the Lord for me. This man grabbed my hands in his. I was already sitting as he knelt down, leaned in, leaned very close to my face, stared directly in my eyes and gave me the same five-minute word as Linda had a few years earlier.

Linda and Dean's prophetic words were so close to one another that I knew they were true. I understood that since God used me to stop these men, all my concerns were laid to rest as I knew it was between them and God. I had so many questions about all these attacks. I could finally put these questions to rest knowing God was in control of those situations all along.

Call to me and I will answer you, and will tell you great and hidden things that you have not known.
(Jeremiah 33:3)

Ask Yourself...

- *How did my childhood prepare me for what God has planned for me now in adulthood?*
- *How can I use even the traumatic experiences to help others who may have experienced similar situations?*
- *What skills have I used to help others?*
- *Have I stepped in and helped someone in need only to find out later it was God who led me to do so?*

-44-

Mysteries Exposed

First Mystery

It was no coincidence that after I started writing this testimony I read Joshua 10:24 for a women's Bible study assignment. I had never noticed this scripture before, but it seemed to be further proof that God used me to stop these evildoers.

Joshua told the commanders of his army, *"Come near; put your feet on the necks of these kings."*

Those were evil kings that God wanted dead by Joshua's hands. This was a common military practice in that day that symbolized the victor's dominion over his captives. The light came on in my head when I read these words.

Reading Joshua gave me a new revelation. These men planned for me to be their next victim. God gave me the victory. God's plan was that these abusive hunters of women became my prey. Not knowing this at the time, the Lord guided me to place my foot on the tall man's neck to be revealed years later as further proof God put me in that situation. One more piece of the puzzle had been added!

We speak the wisdom of God in a mystery, the hidden wisdom which God ordained before the ages of our glory.
(1 Corinthians 2:7)

... in demonstration of the Spirit and of power...
(1 Corinthians 2:4)

Second Mystery

In life, in visions, or whenever I pray for someone, God seems to highlight which way people are facing, either left or right. During my whole life, the left or right position seemed significant though I never knew why. A few years ago, this mystery was revealed by the Spirit.

The Spirit explained in a vision that those who face left indicates that person was still on their journey in life heading toward God. Facing right means their spiritual journey has stopped or possibly ended by their own choosing and by their bad choices. I see this as basic sin and rebellion.

I left all these men crumpled on the ground facing left other than one man. That one man was still in God's hands even though I don't know the end results and probably don't want to know. All these men were severely beaten with many broken bones and none of them were able to walk away on their own accord, much less move. After that season, I haven't seen one woman being abused by a man.

But God has revealed them to us through His Spirit. For the Spirit searches all things, yes, the deep things of God.
(1 Corinthians 2:10)

It makes me happy to know that these two rapists/torturers/murderers who wanted to attack me have or will repent for their evil ways as God repurposes their existence. I understand this is true for them all and that is my answer why the Lord stopped me short of killing them.

Remembering that I moved the tall man by the pant legs a few feet from the other man, I lined them up perfectly for some reason. I wanted them both to face my left. I now realize it was God who gave me this subtle instruction and one I wouldn't understand until years later.

I see this as another confirmation that God put me in front of all those men. God chose me to be there at that time and place and used me as an instrument of violence which was the only language these men understood at the time. Violence and pain toward women was their sport of choice. The Spirit told me each of those ten men's reign of terror was over for good.

I've often wondered if those broken men woke up with a jolt in the middle of the night in the hospital and were haunted by my image in the dark. The worldly side of me hopes so. The godly side of me hopes that as well.

As it reads in Exodus 34, God is gracious and merciful, slow to anger, has a steadfast love for us and forgives our sins. I had none of these qualities when it came to these men. I broke them and laid them out flat in the harshest manner possible.

God was intentional about His strategic plan with regards to all those men. The Spirit showed me through visions that He met those men on the other side of the beatings offering the gift of salvation, forgiveness and a loving relationship with our merciful Lord. The Spirit sent other bold followers of Jesus willing to step up to the task of ministering to them in all their brokenness.

God used their failed attempts to crack open the hardened shells they placed over their hearts as they hoped to shield themselves from their own emotional pain from their past. The Lord squeezed their hearts a little making them uncomfortable through their emotional and physical brokenness. Rendering them vulnerable through their brokenness in spirit, soul and body, it is my prayer they were repentant and open to hear about Jesus.

My God-given appointment is to now stand in prayer for those men hoping the vast chasm between them and God grows closer. The Lord wants to bring them all to repentance on their knees, so they can genuinely proclaim that Jesus is Lord!

… at the name of Jesus every knee should bow, of those in heaven, and of those on earth, and of those under the earth, and that every tongue should confess that Jesus Christ is Lord, to the glory of God the Father. (Philippians 2:10,11)

Ask Yourself...

- *Has God used me to orchestrate a scene that later led to the repentance of another?*
- *Do I see that God can use what others meant for evil for good and to glorify God?*
- *Can I remember a time when I have taken action only to have God reveal later that He gently led me?*
- *What happened and what were the end results?*
- *If that circumstance presented itself again, would I take the same actions not knowing the outcome?*

Answers

Questions? We've all been hurt in life. We all have questions about why some escaped tragedy when others had to endure extreme hardships. The only answer I can offer is for you to surrender your will, your heart and your life to Jesus. Do this through a prayer of salvation and ask God for answers.

If you haven't already done so, your time is now and God is here with you right now and is eager and ready to receive you. He is waiting to love you, bless you and gently lead you to all truth.

Speak these words out loud when you say the prayer of salvation – *Father God, Jesus and Holy Spirit, I surrender my life to you. I believe Jesus gave His life on the cross to pay the ultimate price for all my sins. I believe Father God raised Jesus from the dead. Please forgive me for all my sins.*

I accept Jesus Christ as my Lord and Savior and when I die I will enter Heaven for eternity because You love me so much. In the name of Jesus, I pray. Amen!

Praise God! You are now part of the kingdom of God. The next step is to connect in fellowship at a Bible believing church, read the Bible, pray out loud and ask God all your questions.

Every time I share a testimony it sparks a memory from the listener. I listen as they share a story or two of their lives they didn't understand before, sometimes chalking it up to coincidence. Coincidences are the labels people attach to unexplained occurrences when they don't recognize God's hand in their own lives. My intent is to shift people's awareness that we have all heard the voice of God or have witnessed His hand in our lives blessing us with many miracles.

We aren't to put God in a box. His ways are not our ways. God can use any situation to reveal His presence in our lives. He often does, but we need to be watchful, aware and thankful when we see God's handiwork in our lives.

My goal is to revive and answer those questions you've had lying dormant in your past. It is my hope I have offered you compelling evidence of God's powerful love in your life as you remember similar encounters from your own past.

I pray this second book, *Bragging About God Again: Holy Spirit Encounters,* has brought you even closer to the God of the Universe. I pray that as you read through my personal struggles and challenges you will see how God gave me what I needed, not only to survive these troubling times, but to thrive in them. I hope you realize God wants to do the same for you.

The Lord is my shepherd;
I shall not want.
He makes me to lie down in green pastures;
He leads me beside the still waters.
He restores my soul;
He leads me in the paths of righteousness
For His name's sake.
Yea, though I walk through the valley of the shadow of death,
I will fear no evil;
For You are with me;
Your rod and Your staff, they comfort me.
You prepare a table before me in the presence of my enemies;
You anoint my head with oil;
My cup runs over.
Surely goodness and mercy shall follow me
All the days of my life,
And I will dwell in the house of the Lord
Forever.
Amen!
(Psalms 23:1-6)

Ready for more?

Please visit my website *BraggingAboutGod.com* to read more complete information on God's Health Protocol mentioned in Chapter 21 Cancer Answer.

To purchase Joni Jones' first book, *Bragging About God: Hearing His Voice* please go to -

Xulonpress.com/bookstore
Amazon.com
BarnesandNoble.com

CPSIA information can be obtained
at www.ICGtesting.com
Printed in the USA
LVOW10s0032270118

564198LV00001B/1/P